PHYSICAL CONTACT IN EDUCATIONAL SETTINGS

PHYSICAL CONTACT IN EDUCATIONAL SETTINGS

JOACIM ANDERSSON, ANNICA CALDEBORG, AND MARIE ÖHMAN

First published in 2025
as part of **Sports & Society Book Imprint**
Common Ground Research Networks
University of Illinois Research Park
2001 South First St, Suite 201 L
Champaign, IL 61820 USA

Copyright © Andersson, Joacim, Caldeborg, Annica, Öhman, Marie, 2025

All rights reserved. Apart from fair dealing for the purposes of study, research, criticism or review as permitted under the applicable copyright legislation, no part of this book may be reproduced by any process without written permission from the publisher.

Library of Congress Cataloging-in-Publication Data

Names: Andersson, Joacim, author. | Caldeborg, Annica, author. | Öhman, Marie, author.
Title: Physical contact in educational settings / Joacim Andersson, Annica Caldeborg, Marie Öhman.
Description: Champaign, IL : Common Ground Research Networks, 2025. | Includes bibliographical references. | Summary: "Researchers and educators in physical education have experienced a rapid change when it comes to bodily norms and values. Today, we are much more cautious and conscious about how we navigate intimacy in general and physical contact in particular. Such changes are experienced through the immediacy of bodily engagement in teaching and learning. Hence, how and to what extent we put our body and our personal selves at risk in teaching situations have been called into question. The embodied means and outcomes we rely on in realizing our educational vision has undergone transformation. Adaption to such changes and transformations need to be explicitly identified and discussed among PE educators, PE teachers, pre-school teachers and students as well as sport coaches and athletes. In this book we have collected, selected and synthesized what we found valuable and important about physical contact between adults and children in educational settings"-- Provided by publisher.
Identifiers: LCCN 2024059376 (print) | LCCN 2024059377 (ebook) | ISBN 9781966214168 (paperback) | ISBN 9781966214175 (adobe pdf)
Subjects: LCSH: Physical education and training--Methodology. | Physical education and training--Moral and ethical aspects. | Interaction analysis in education.
Classification: LCC GV342 .A525 2025 (print) | LCC GV342 (ebook) | DDC 796.071--dc23/eng/20250115
LC record available at https://lccn.loc.gov/2024059376
LC ebook record available at https://lccn.loc.gov/2024059377

ISBN: 978-1-966214-16-8 (PBK)
ISBN: 978-1-966214-17-5 (pdf)
DOI: 10.18848/978-1-966214-17-5/CGP

Cover Image: Joline Andersson

SPORT & SOCIETY POCKETBOOK TEACHING SERIES

The Sport and Society Pocketbook Teaching Series aims to introduce students and a general readership to relevant topics, theories, and concepts within sport history and sport sociology. The topics will vary but are united in their purpose to serve as an accessible alternative to generic textbook offerings or academic research monographs. We hope that the shorter and more accessible pocketbook format of the series will mean that each book can be read in an hour or two on a quiet evening or while commuting on a bus or train. This aligns with our ethos of accessibility in scholarly communication. Books in the series can be accessed in print and electronic formats. In addition, and in parallel to both editions, each title will be accompanied by an online repository where additional learning and teaching resources are provided. The electronic platform for the series will include links to recent and significant research articles, visual materials, podcasts, lectures, and more, thus securing ongoing relevance by providing new and engaging resources and perspectives aligned with the topic of each book. This series is for teachers, learners, and individuals with an interest in sports alike.

Dr. Jörg Krieger (Aarhus University, Denmark)
Dr. April Henning (Heriot-Watt University, United Kingdom)
Dr. Lindsay Parks Pieper (University of Lynchburg, United States)
Dr. Jesper Andreasson (Linnaeus University, Sweden)

Table of Contents

Chapter 1: An incident and some confusions 1
Discourse and physical contact 5
Purpose and chapter disposition... 7
Questions to discuss.. 11

Chapter 2: The rise of physical contact as a field of research 13
The child protection discourse 13
Physical contact – a pedagogical tool 15
The development of the research field... 16
Summary... 20
Questions to discuss.. 21

Chapter 3: Physical Contact and teachers' strategies 23
Theoretical and methodological considerations........................ 23
Pedagogical consequences of touching or no-touch
in PE teachers' practical work.. 26
Effects on PE teachers work... 27
Pedagogically relevant physical contact in PE 28
Teaching strategies in relation to physical contact.................... 33
Physical Education teachers' professionalism............................ 37
Questions to discuss.. 39

Chapter 4: Physical contact and teaching techniques 41
Body pedagogics and techniques of physical contact............. 43
Embodied teaching values 45
Teaching as a caring profession..46
Three different techniques of physical contact..........................50
Summary 58
Questions to discuss..60

Chapter 5: Physical contact and student reflexivity 61
The didactic contract...62
Physical contact – a matter of negotiations 64
Summary 72
Questions to discuss..74

Chapter 6: The Future – with or without physical contact... 75
Revisiting our initial concerns...77
Closing notes 81
Further readings..84

Notes *87*

References *89*

CHAPTER 1

An Incident and Some Confusions

As researchers and teacher educators in physical education (PE), we have experienced a rather rapid change when it comes to bodily norms and values. Today, we are much more cautious and conscious about how we navigate intimacy in general and physical contact in particular. Such changes are experienced through the immediacy of bodily engagement in teaching and learning. Hence, how and to what extent we put our body and our personal selves at risk in teaching situations have been called into question. The embodied means and outcomes we rely on in realizing our educational vision have undergone transformation. Adaptations to such changes and transformations need to be explicitly identified and discussed among PE educators, PE teachers, preschool teachers and students, as well as sport coaches and athletes. In this book, we have collected, selected, and synthesized what we found valuable and important about physical contact between adults and children in educational settings.

As researchers, we always find it difficult to point out eureka moments or disclosing an exact place and point in time for where and when certain ideas occurred for the first time. However, there is one event that initially inspired us strongly and that has continued to influence our thoughts and interests of physical contact between adults and children in education. The collected experiences among us as authors amounts to some forty years of teaching in physical education teacher education (PETE).

Among other things, we have taught gymnastics, dance, motor skill movements, and outdoor activities. Ten years ago, a new and unexpected topic of conversation surfaced during a lesson in PETE, where gymnastics and acrobatics were on the agenda. The students were practicing handstands, cartwheels, and different kinds of vaulting exercises on a mini trampoline. An important part of the lesson was how to physically assist and support these movements in order to help each other cope with the exercises and to minimize the risk of injury—an essential learning before the upcoming professional role. The students were also doing acrobatics and "body pyramids," standing on each other's shoulders, which necessitated close physical contact with each other. At the end of the lesson, students were massaging each other's shoulders as a way of relieving muscle tension. When the lesson was finished one of the students said: "When I become a PE teacher, I'll never do any of the things we have done in class today." When asked to explain this quite surprising announcement, the student's response was: "You can't touch pupils today, they might think I'm a paedophile or a 'dirty old man.'" Many of the other students supported and emphasized these worries and gave various reasons for how this type of teaching would be difficult to perform with children and young people. Since that lesson, we have continued to ask ourselves: *When, how, and why could supporting a student attempting handstands and acrobatic movements be interpreted as sexual harassment or sexual abuse?* It also made us wonder what consequences and long-standing effects such thoughts and feelings will have on teaching and learning and what transformation processes this will generate when it comes to PE teachers' professionalism.

The event above gives us insights to a general problem in society, namely, the complex issue of physical contact between adults and children in educational settings where bodies are guided, corrected, and indeed touched with the intention of enabling physical capabilities, performance, learning, and development. It raises several important societal, pedagogical, and moral questions. In the beginning when we first experienced these phenomena in our teaching, we neither had the understanding nor the scientific facts or practical tools to properly guide students in navigating this intimacy minefield of teaching PE. Today, challenges concerning physical contact between adults and children are probably even more intricate, although we are better supported by recent sport pedagogy research on intergenerational touch. Our hope is that some of this knowledge can serve as effective tools for practitioners, educators, students, and researchers in their call to teach/coach and their quest for sound pedagogically learning environments.

Even though all examples in the book are taken from the school subject Physical Education,[1] they are also relevant for other areas, for example, teachers of other school subjects, preschool teachers, sport coaches, or professionals in other occupations where physical contact is used, such as nurses and carers for older people. The starting point for this book was a return to our PE teachers' and students' thoughts and feelings about the critical aspects of physical contact in PE teaching. As we were confused and somewhat frustrated by the above incident, we identified three concerns that supplied further guidance for how we outlined the book.

(i) We began to understand that the changes our students described did not come from within the field of PE teachers, PE syllabus, or PE research. Instead, what our students experienced was an amplified sensibility for how we, as a professional group, were looked upon from the outside and how our professional duties were crossfired by social norms and values and public debates in fundamentally new ways. This reflects a problem of corrosion of teacher professionalism that must be critically examined and explained.

(ii) We began to feel that the fundamental embodied basis for engaging in the PE profession had changed. One of our most familiar pedagogical tools, physical contact, had been threatened. There appeared to be a gap, whereby physical contact as a pedagogical tool worked in PETE but, according to our students, not out in the schools.

(iii) We began to see that the worry of being mistrusted or accused of sexual harassment was about PE teachers' fears. Our PETE students' unwillingness to use physical contact in their future teaching, as well as the evident clash between certain social norms and values and physical contact as a professional pedagogical tool, has led us to realize that we also need a student perspective on this issue. How do students experience physical contact in teaching situations and do the students share the teachers' vulnerability and anxiety?

These concerns have influenced how we through the years have pursued different research projects on which we now build the different chapters. In this way, the concerns constitute the driving force throughout the book. Even though our experiences were from a gym class, we understood that our concerns were related to wider social changes and various educational settings. We understood these changes in terms of a new discourse around child protection and physical contact between teachers and students in educational settings. The term discourse will be a recurring term in the book; therefore, we want to briefly describe what we mean by a discourse and also how societal discourses have changed when it comes to physical contact between teachers and students in educational settings.

Discourse and Physical Contact

A discourse is a certain way of talking about and understanding the world, or a part of it (Winther-Jörgensen & Philips, 2000). A discourse can also be understood as a system of representation. This means that a discourse is "a group of statements which provide a language for talking about a particular topic" (Hall, 2004, p. 72). People's way of talking about a topic, for example physical contact, is in other words not a neutral image of reality. Discourses can facilitate certain ways of talking and acting in relation to physical contact in education, while limiting other ways of talking and acting about the same topic.

When it comes to PE teachers' work, physical contact was and is, for many, still regarded as necessary and important for students' learning, development, and growth. Children need help the first time they try a handstand, ride a bike or when they learn how to swim. This has been the dominating discourse, something that people have generally accepted and agreed on, and therefore find it hard to question. More recently, however, physical contact has also come to be viewed as something that can be risky for adults and children in educational settings. The adult offering the help may have insincere intentions; therefore, physical contact should be avoided. The child protection discourse, policies, and guidelines for the safety of children is about eliminating risks and creating safe environments for children and adults in educational settings. This creates a new discourse, which entails various consequences for teachers, students, and subject content.

Over the years, teachers have developed habits in teaching. A discourse is created that enables physical contact in learning situations and for children's development and growth—something obvious and necessary. When new ways of speaking and acting in relation to physical contact are established, discourses clash with each other. Thus, the knowledge and the new ways of speaking about a phenomenon influence teachers' behavior and habits. If we return to our handstand example in the introduction, two different discourses are clashing when we are forced to ask ourselves if we should support a handstand or not. Who, and what, decides what is right or wrong? This condition of clashing discourses means that teachers must balance between the heightened concern for children's welfare, existing teaching traditions, and practical knowledge.

An issue that has heightened the concern for children's welfare is reports in, for instance, media of sexual harassment and abuse in church, in the scouting movement, in sports, or in school settings against children. Guidelines and policies containing restrictions or recommendations of appropriate or inappropriate physical contact have been put in place with the good intention of protecting children from harm. The problem, however, is that such guidelines and policies have also had some unexpected consequences. For instance, practitioners who work with children and whose main goal is to act in the children's best interest have started to express feelings of anxiety and fear (Lawrence, 2004; Öhman, 2017). They have become uncertain as to how physical contact can or should be used in appropriate ways without risking being suspected of malpractice or improper behavior. We know that teachers experience an increased level of anxiety concerning specifically physical contact between adults and children or young people (Andrzejewski & Davis, 2008; Fletcher, 2013; Johnson, 2015; Jones, 2004; Öhman, 2017; Piper & Smith, 2003; Piper et al., 2013b). We also know that an avoidance of touching a child is increasingly justified by referring to the children's rights agenda. The anxiety teachers and other professionals who work with children can experience is mainly due to fears related to the risk of being suspected of, or falsely accused of, sexual harassment or molestation (Fletcher, 2013; Jones, 2004; Piper et al., 2013b). To be a little more concrete, it can be about a teacher's or coach's concern about how to give a child a helping hand when doing a somersault, or how to support a body in motion. In these and similar situations, the support can easily end up just slightly wrong. It can be a matter of centimeters for something to be perceived as inappropriate by the child, a spectator or by oneself, and there are invisible borders that indicate where, how, and why a physical support is appropriate or not. Is it OK to help a student to do a handstand by holding on to their legs and hips, or is it OK to comfort a student by giving them a hug or by letting them sit in the teacher's lap? To spot a student doing a midair flip entails being ready to catch or take hold of a moving body at high speed—what happens if the teacher catches/grabs the student a few centimeters off the intended place on the body? Perhaps the teacher touches the breasts to prevent an over-rotation. Is that inappropriate? And if so, to whom? For some, these described situations are clear-cut. Either physical contact is seen as natural and necessary, an obvious and expected part of teaching and coaching, or these situations fall into a gray area, which can cause anxiety as to whether the situation can be deemed appropriate.

Purpose and Chapter Disposition

To begin with, we must emphasize that a right to be protected from sexual or other abuse is indeed a human right for all people. While we do not wish to diminish the importance of dealing with problems of abuse, harm, and sexual harassment, we do want to emphasize the need for reflections and alternative perspectives on physical contact in educational settings. The overall aim of the book is to contribute to the understanding of the phenomenon of physical contact in educational settings, and present and discuss certain tools and concepts that are useful in analyzing pedagogical practices in relation to physical contact. The chapters relate to different projects we, as researchers in the field, have carried out. In each chapter, we address physical contact from a different perspective, which means that we use different theoretical concepts and different data from our research projects. In chapter two, we summarize and explain the scope of available research literature and identify main themes in the research field of intergenerational touch. We then proceed through three chapters that describe and discuss teachers' strategies (chap 3), teachers' techniques (chap 4), and students' reflexivity (chap 5) in relation to physical contact. These three chapters represent different perspectives on how we can think critically about physical contact and discuss teachers' and students' experiences of this. Finally, in chapter six, we reflect on pedagogical practices in general and suggest three different types of embodiment work that we as pedagogues and researchers should consider in order to create good learning environments in an era where no-touch discourses prevail. In the chapter disposition below, we further outline the contents of each chapter and how they differ.

In chapter two, *The rise of physical contact as a field of research,* a brief description of previous research in the research field of intergenerational touch is given. Intergenerational touch and physical contact are not two different names for the same thing. The term intergenerational touch refers to the field of research that focuses on physical contact between adults and children in educational settings. For example, the relationship between teacher and student, sports coaches and athletes, or preschool teachers and children. The chapter gives an overview of the development of this specific field and describes some main themes highlighted in research and some factors that have influenced the creation of a no-touch culture.

In chapter three, *Physical Contact and teachers' strategies*, we turn to teachers with knowledge and experience of PE practice and discuss how they reflect on physical contact and their professionalism. This chapter builds on a research project on interviews with PE teachers. Three practice-based arguments that support the use of physical contact in PE are presented. By using Foucault's work (1978/1991, 1982/2002) on dominating discourses in society, we show how a child protection discourse impacts the teaching situation in terms of facilitating or restraining actions. By using Foucault's concept of self-governance questions can be posed about how arguments, norms, and values relate to no-touch discourses and what strategies that teachers have developed for dealing with physical contact in their teaching. It is notable that teachers are experiencing increased social control. They struggle with higher levels of insecurity and vagueness and have become more aware of the possible consequences of touching students. In the chapter, we problematize how teachers' knowledge, habits, and professional identity are at risk and how certain traditional activities may include an increased risk-taking in some teaching situations.

In chapter four, *Physical contact and teaching techniques*, we build on interview data where PE teachers talked about encounters with students that resulted in certain tensions for them. Against this background, we argue that to understand issues regarding physical contact we must conceive it as deeply associated with specific teaching techniques. We pick up Nodding's notions of caring to consider teaching as a caring profession. Caring, as a practical teacher concern, requires wisdom regarding the right time to use physical contact and to refrain from such use. From a body pedagogical perspective, we approach physical contact between teachers and students as an essential tension. We deal with the tension embedded in the paradox of caring that PE teachers not only risk their freedom by being potentially accused of sexual harassment but also their embodied teaching techniques and their very teaching selves. Thus, using the concepts "body pedagogics" and "care" allows us to move from looking at physical contact as a discursive and power-related problem to rather understanding it as an embodied teaching technique through which teachers handle caring relationships at different levels. The concepts of "body pedagogics" and "care" thereby open up for an understanding of PE teachers' profession as a shared cultural knowledge about how to navigate intimacy in teaching.

In chapter five, *Physical contact and student reflexivity,* we focus on what the students say about physical contact. The chapter builds on a three-year project that conducted group interviews with physical education students. The students' experience of physical contact is understood through didactic theory and the concept of the didactic contract, which implies an unspoken agreement in the relationship between teachers and students in teaching practice. The didactic contract, as a concept, facilitates critical questions about the confidence that must be established between teacher and student to make learning possible, and how that process relates to physical contact as a teaching phenomenon. For example, when is the didactic contract at risk of being broken in situations where physical contact occurs? Students' experiences illustrate that PE teaching would not be possible without students' well-reflected attitudes about physical contact. Just as teachers find confidence in their embodied teaching techniques and habits of caring, students find confidence in their reflexive approaches to different teacher behaviors and purpose of activities. The chapter also deals with gender and cultural differences regarding physical contact between teacher and students in the teaching situations.

In chapter six, *The Future—with or without physical contact,* we conclude the different chapters and discuss our above concerns and relate these to the main concepts we used in different chapters. We discuss the use of physical contact in relation to PE teachers, students, and the subject content. We highlight the complexity of being a PE teacher, or any occupation with children and young people, where you often will be at the crossroads of policy, practice, theory, youth culture, and social discourses. Lastly, we suggest value-building work, embodiment work, and relational work as three areas that need pedagogic efforts to call into existence the good of our practices.

Questions to Discuss

- What does a discourse mean? Identify some societal discourses related to the body that you recognize in your daily life. In what way do you or people around you contribute to these discourses? How are these discourses challenged (if at all)?
- How do you understand the term intergenerational touch? In what different contexts can you relate to the term intergenerational touch?

CHAPTER 2

The Rise of Physical Contact as a Field of Research[1]

In this chapter, we want to give the reader a picture of what research has shown in the field of intergenerational touch related to physical contact between children and adults in educational settings. This background is important in order to understand the complexity of the field and how the field of research has several different and sometimes conflicting perspectives. Important to remember here is that intergenerational touch refers to the research field as such, while physical contact refers to the phenomenon that we focus on in an educational setting.

The Child Protection Discourse

The research field of intergenerational touch has emerged from the child protection discourse (Lawrence, 2004). In the child protection discourse, the child is seen as mainly vulnerable and in need of protection. The child protection discourse is said to be the result of the "discovery" of child abuse in the 1960s. It may seem odd to talk about the "discovery" of child abuse as late as the 1960s since children of all times have been subjected to abuse from adults. It was, however, not until now that the concept of child abuse came about. In the beginning, child abuse was mainly seen as a medical and scientific problem (Lawrence, 2004). One example of this is the publication of "The Battered-Child Syndrome" (Kempe et al., 1985), where children who had been subjected to serious physical abuse by a parent or foster parent were identified (Kempe et al., 1985). From the more medical approach in the 1960s, child abuse eventually became acknowledged as a social problem that fundamentally changed the view of children in society. If the medical approach identified clinical signs of abuse, the new order instead identified risks of abuse, and child abuse management was superseded by the child protection discourse (Lawrence, 2004, p. 72). It was also the protection of children that formed the basis for the children's rights movement, and in discussions about children's rights, it is mainly the protection of children that is in focus (Öhman & Quennerstedt, 2017). This means that children are seen as being in need of protection from many risks. Policies and guidelines have thus been created to protect children and young people from being subjected to abuse (Brackenridge, 2001; Fasting, 2005; Toftegaard Nielsen, 2001). In many cases, these policies and guidelines include recommendations for how adults should behave or act toward children, and where a restricted use of physical contact is often recommended. For example: *When a child is upset, try to seek ways to provide comfort and support without unnecessary or excessive physical contact* (The World Organization of the Scout Movement European Region/World Association of Girl Guides and Girl Scouts (WAGGGS), 2007, p. 8). In other words, physical contact has come to be viewed as a threat to the security of children. This example shows how a new way of speaking about physical contact is constructed—a new discourse that talks about physical contact in a different way and that clashes with another accepted language about physical contact in educational settings: Should I, or should I not, have physical contact with my students?

Here, we come back to the child protection discourse and the "new" talk about children's safety and safe environments. We all agree that the environments where children spend their time, whether it be home, school or recreational places, should be safe spaces for them. Children have always needed safe environments, but this has not been recognized or talked about in this particular way before. The fact that we today talk about this in a clear way has many consequences. In educational settings, creating a safe environment for children and for teachers has in many places come to be characterized by no touching (Fletcher, 2013; Jones, 2004; Öhman & Quennerstedt, 2017). When our talk about a certain topic is intensified, we usually learn more about that topic. But at the same time, problems are revealed that must be dealt with in various ways. That is the reason why we can see consequences of the talk about physical contact, a new discourse in policies, in interpersonal meetings, in cultural practices and educational settings.

Physical Contact—A Pedagogical Tool

In the previous section, it was shown that policies and guidelines put in place for the protection of children often include recommendations for the use of physical contact between adults and children. A legitimate question to ask is when and for what reason physical contact is needed or used in educational settings. Research about physical contact in educational settings supports the general assumption that physical contact is necessary for children's development and that it would be more harmful for children to receive too little physical contact (Öhman & Quennerstedt, 2017; Piper et al., 2012, p. 332). It has been shown that physical contact can have calming effects on preschool children and that it can help develop children's well-being (Svinth, 2018). In addition, physical contact is used by teachers in PE to help students to "get it right." This can involve getting the right feeling for a specific bodily movement or performing a movement correctly or learning how to avoid injuries (Andersson et al., 2018; Öhman & Quennerstedt, 2017). Fletcher (2013, p. 701) says: "Basic athletic instruction necessitates contact." Physical contact is also used to prevent injuries, create good relationships between adults and children in educational settings, and establish good learning conditions (Öhman & Quennerstedt, 2017). It is also used to deal with social situations, such as manners or behavior, and to express care as a human necessity. For instance, Jung and Choi (2016, p. 132) claim that "a single touch can be more meaningful than a thousand words."

Development of the Research Field

So far, we have learnt that physical contact in educational settings between adults and children has become risky behavior for educators who may be suspected of abuse if they use physical contact in their teaching. Codes of conduct put in place to protect children from harm have in other words contributed to a situation where many adults who work with children have become afraid of using physical contact as a pedagogical tool. The research field of intergenerational touch is in general terms a fairly new field of research. In order to get a glimpse of the development of this field, we turn to a review article by Caldeborg et al. (2023). An interesting development is the steady growth in the number of published texts on the issue from the beginning of the new millennium. In fact, before 2000, there were almost no articles on the topic published. During the last twenty years, the number of published articles related to physical contact between adults and children in educational settings has steadily increased, both in terms of the number of articles, the number of journals as well as the number of countries where the studies have been conducted. The countries represented are generally Western, although some other countries/regions are also represented, such as Saudi Arabia and Central Africa (see Caldeborg et al., 2023 for a more detailed overview).

Year	2000–2009	2010–2015	2016–2022
Number of articles (60)	13	22	25
Countries (16)	8	8	10
Journals (36)	12	11	17

(Adapted from Caldeborg et al., 2023)

One of the reasons for the increase of published articles in recent years is of course the heightened interest in society concerning child safety. Several research projects, in the UK and in Sweden, focusing on physical contact in PE, sports coaching and in preschool were launched during this period, and generated many articles on the topic. The authors of the review conclude that certain research topics in the field have so far prevailed over others.

The most prevailing perspective is clearly being critical toward no-touch policies and guidelines. The reason for this critical stance is generally the claim that the needs of children are lost as no-touch policies and guidelines risk leading to less physical contact in educational settings. The arguments are that children need physical contact to develop as persons as well as to acquire skills in movement activities. The critical stance is also due to fears and anxieties among teachers and coaches in these settings who use physical contact as a pedagogical tool in their daily work—fears that are related to the risk of being falsely accused of inappropriate behavior. In line with this, the critical perspective also has shown that the professional identity of teachers, who regularly use physical contact as a pedagogical tool, has been bruised in that they now have started to question themselves and their roles. For instance, Garratt et al. (2013) claim that the professional use of physical contact in PE and sports coaching has come to be viewed as malpractice rather than pedagogy. At the same time, as professionals experience an increased level of fear or anxiety of using physical contact, there are also educators who are critical to the no-touch policies, and act in what they perceive is in the best interest of those they teach (Jones et al., 2013) regardless of policies or guidelines. For instance, older and more experienced educators seem to be less inclined to adhere blindly to the child protection discourse and its codes of conduct, while younger and less experienced PE teachers and coaches to a greater extent accept the policies and the recommendations proposed by guidelines (Piper et al., 2013a, 2013b). Another example are institutions who have refused to have in place written guidelines, arguing that they are not practical and even unnecessary (Piper & Stronach, 2008, p. 46). It is generally not the practitioners themselves who have written or decided upon guidelines relating to physical contact, and that can be one reason why resistance against such guidelines can be found among some of them. However, even if opportunities for resistance exist among practitioners, the pressure on them to adhere to norms and policies related to the use of physical contact in educational settings is often very strong (Taylor et al., 2016). That is, it is not easy to resist norms and policies put in place for the protection of children, even if they are unrealistic or impractical in the actual educational setting.

Alongside these very critical studies within the research field, there are also studies that have focused on, for example, gender and/or cultural differences. In terms of gender differences, research has shown that male professionals seem to feel that they are more at risk of being accused of improper behavior than their female counterparts (Åberg et al., 2019; Caldeborg, 2022; Caldeborg & Öhman, 2020). The perspective of cultural differences has revealed variations in acceptable ways of using physical contact between, and also within, cultures or religions. Gender and cultural differences are in addition some of the issues that are brought up in studies that acknowledge students' experiences and reflections on physical contact.

Researchers in the field of intergenerational touch generally agree that physical contact previously was regarded as quite straightforward and taken for granted in the subject of PE or in sports coaching. However, a change in attitude has taken place, and physical contact has instead become a risky behavior (Fletcher, 2013; Öhman, 2017; Taylor et al., 2016). As a result, some practitioners have changed the way they use physical contact. For example, instead of touching a student with an open hand, which could be interpreted as a form of caress, some have instead started to touch their students with a clenched hand (Öhman, 2017).

When guidelines that restrict the use of physical contact are linked to children's right's to be protected from harm, they also become difficult to criticize. Of course, the right to be protected from any form of abuse is a basic human right for all people indeed, but as pedagogues, we need to continue the discussion about what consequences an overprotective view of children, and adults, can lead to in educational settings.

Summary

In this chapter, we have learned about the development of the research field intergenerational touch. It has its roots in the child protection discourse, where children are foremost seen as vulnerable and in need of protection. Policies and guidelines often recommend limited physical contact between adults and children in educational settings. A consequence of these policies and guidelines is that professionals who use physical contact as a pedagogical tool in their daily work have become fearful and anxious of how their use of physical contact may be perceived by others. They also fear being falsely accused of sexual harassment. It is also noteworthy that the "no-touch" policy has been received differently in Western societies and that concerns about physical contact between adults and children in educational settings vary in different countries (Piper et al., 2013a). Since the 1990s, researchers in Anglo-Saxon countries have warned of a media-driven moral panic regarding contact between educators and children (Piper & Smith, 2003). In many Anglo-Saxon countries, educators have an explicit and written no-touch policy to follow. It is important to note that a "no-touch policy" is not a legally enforced document but a set of guidelines and recommendations. Although it is not illegal to touch students in school, research has increasingly shown and taken interest in teachers' growing uncertainties about physical contact with students.

In this book, the empirical material is taken from the Swedish school subject Physical Education (PE). Therefore, it is important to emphasize that Swedish PE teachers do not have a written "no-touch policy" to follow, but the documents do exist within for example, the sports movement and the scouting movement. The "no-touch policy" is probably less pervasive in Sweden than it is, for example, in the UK and the US. The body culture in Sweden has been described as relatively liberal which may be one of the reasons why Swedish debates about physical contact in education are relatively new but increasingly influential (Hedlin, 2021).

Even though touching students in school is not illegal, documents and recommendations create a "no-touch discourse," which includes safeguarding, suspicion, and fear. The concept of discourse is thus used to describe conditions that are so dominant that they appear inevitable. The power of discourse (Foucault, 1978/1991) here means that teachers act in relation to what is regarded as generally expected, what seems good and right. Even if the Swedish PE teachers do not have a "no-touch policy" to follow, the discourse about no-touch is so strong that they experience a dilemma as to whether and when it is justified and reasonable to touch students (Varea & Öhman, 2023).

Many studies in the research field are critical to "no-touch" policies and guidelines. The arguments are that the needs of children are at risk of being lost, and that "no-touch" would become the new norm in educational settings. It is suggested in research that physical contact is important for a child's movement development, and for the establishment of good relationships, learning conditions and as an expression of care. This is, however, a complex and difficult issue, since it is difficult to criticize recommendations for the protection of children without being seen as insensitive.

Questions to Discuss

- What are your own experiences of physical contact in educational settings? List some opportunities and difficulties.
- What arguments can be raised for or against the use of physical contact in educational settings?

CHAPTER 3

Physical Contact and Teachers' Strategies[1]

In the previous chapters, we have highlighted that several scholars have explored how the production of a "safe child" and a "safe teacher" has become a dominant feature of the everyday work in educational settings (Fletcher, 2013; Jones, 2004; Öhman, 2017; Ohman & Grundberg Sandell, 2015; Piper, 2015b; Piper et al., 2013a, 2013b). Based on a risk perspective, no touch at all seems to be the solution to create security for all parties involved.[2] In this chapter, we turn to physical education (PE) teachers and listen to what they have to say about physical contact in their teaching. More specifically, the chapter deals with how PE teachers are affected by the child protection discourse and no-touch policies. How do they handle physical contact with the students, and what strategies have they developed when it comes to physical contact in teaching situations? We draw on interview data from 23 PE teachers' (10 women and 13 men) aged between 30 and 63 and at different stages in their careers. The teachers worked in a total of 15 different Swedish primary, secondary and upper secondary schools in urban and rural areas.[3]

Theoretical and Methodological Considerations

The study takes its starting point in a discourse-analytical tradition using a methodology based on Foucault's ideas about dominating discourses and self-governance. Discourses in a Foucauldian way can be understood as regular language rules that allow certain statements and actions to be made in an obvious way. When we talk about a dominant discourse, we mean that a certain way of thinking and acting is taken for granted and thus rarely questioned. An important question we ask in this chapter is how child protection and no-touch policies impact PE teaching situation in terms of facilitating or restraining actions. By using the concept of a dominating discourse, we can understand how child protection and no-touch policies in society impact the PE teaching situation. This means that it becomes analytically important to examine what is going on in practice.

By using the concept of self-governance, we can also present some strategies that teachers have developed for dealing with physical contact in their teaching. Self-governance is a theoretical concept used to describe a form of self-regulation, where, without coercion, people act in relation to that which is regarded as generally right. According to Foucault (1978/1991), self-governance involves the ways in which individuals learn, judge, and regulate themselves in relation to what is generally accepted in a specific discourse. We act in ways that we consider wise and sensible.

The public anxiety that is associated with physical contact between children and adults has also spread to a variety of institutional activities, such as the sports movement, the church, the scout movement, preschool and the school subject PE. Even if many of the discussions about child protection, safeguarding and no-touch arise in specific areas (e.g., sport, scouting, childcare, PE), they should be linked to other connected domains (Garratt et al., 2013). Thus, new ways of talking and acting in a specific area do not only affect the practices in that specific field, but those in other domains as well. This is precisely how we can understand the power of a dominating discourse. Nealon (2008, p. 71) has argued that we should pay attention to those social practices that appear to be beyond question, because "power becomes more effective while offering less obvious potential for resistance." This means that probably none of us would deny that children should be protected from abuse of various kinds. Who would not want their child to be protected and in a safe environment? It is difficult to resist the child protection discourse, which means that the power of the discourse becomes strong and powerful.

The production of child protection policy documents and codes of practice by organizations dealing with children and young people has emerged in recent years. These documents, which aim to create safe environments for children, often include guidelines for appropriate and inappropriate interactions. Some advocate a very restrictive use of physical contact—one of the most explicit examples being the scouting movement's Child Protection Tool Kit: "Where physical contact is necessary, be sensitive and always avoid touching the children and young people yourself," and "When physical contact is unavoidable, ensure that another adult is present" (WOSM/WAGGGS, 2007, p. 8). However, it is not a question of legislation. In most countries, touching students in school is not illegal, but recommendations and policy documents, that is, "no-touch" policies, safeguarding and the promotion of children's rights, are created. It is of course not something we can resist in a simple way, but we must look at the consequences of a "no-touch" culture in educational contexts.

PE teachers must deal with physical contact in one way or another. The relationship between prescribed actions and the individual's own responsibility to act in line with these, can be seen as self-regulation. Rose (1999, p. 11) expresses: "We evaluate ourselves according to the criteria provided for us by others."

According to earlier research, teachers need to be more risk conscious, avoid false accusations of guilt and protect themselves in the teaching situation (Fletcher, 2013; Öhman, 2016; Piper, 2015a; Piper et al., 2013a, 2013b). This facilitates the investigation of how processes of self-regulation are staged in PE teachers' work.

However, even if the child protection discourse is seen as strong and powerful, there is always room for resistance. Foucault (1982/2002, p. 324) says that "there is no power without potential refusal or revolt," which means that resistance can lead to new ways of talking and acting. In the analytical work of the interviews, the focus is on the actions that PE teachers develop when acting in line with or against the child protection discourse and "no-touch" policy. Focusing on teachers' self-regulation makes it also possible to examine the different strategies the teachers have developed regarding physical contact in teaching.

Using a Foucauldian inspired approach makes it possible to reflect on and critically examine the consequences of dominating discourses and how they produce specific ways of thinking and acting, that is, what the consequences might be, in this case for PE teachers' professional work.

Pedagogical Consequences of Touching or No-Touch in PE Teachers' Practical Work

In this section of the chapter, we will try to answer three questions: (i) How has the increased public anxiety associated with physical contact between teachers and students affected teachers work? (ii) In what kind of pedagogical situations do teachers consider physical contact as pedagogically relevant and necessary in PE? (iii) What strategies have teachers developed in relation to physical contact in their teaching?

The first question is presented in the form of a more general nature in terms of how the teachers' work has been affected. Regarding the second question we have identified three practice-based arguments that support the use of physical contact in PE practice: (i) Touching as a precondition for a certain subject content in PE, (ii) Touching as a way of establishing the conditions for learning needed in PE, (iii) Touching as a human necessity and as an expression of care. Each argument focuses on a specific advantage of physical contact between the teacher and the student that is relevant for students' development and learning (see also Öhman & Quennerstedt, 2017). Considering the third question, two different self-regulating strategies are presented: (i) Adaptation using avoidance-oriented strategies and (ii) Resistance using downplaying-oriented strategies. By asking these questions, we can make visible how teachers deal with the issue of physical contact in their teaching and what pedagogical consequences it brings. Thereby, we can discuss the issue of physical contact in teaching situations from different perspectives. The results are presented based on the abovementioned questions.

Effects on PE Teachers' Work

The findings of the study indicate a complex picture. All the interviewed PE teachers declare that physical contact is an important and necessary part of PE and that they are familiar with the child protection discourse and "no-touch" policies. Nevertheless, they relate to physical contact in different ways. On the one hand, and in line with earlier research in other countries, the Swedish PE teachers are anxious about and unsure of how to handle physical contact in teaching situations. It is also apparent that this kind of pressure or fear has increased in recent years. Some teachers, both male and female, express a greater fear than others and say, "It's one of the worst things that could happen to me. Imagine getting a bad reputation or being reported" or "It's a real dilemma and all the write-ups in the paper are scary."

Emotions like fear and worry are related to getting a bad reputation or being accused of any form of molestation. Regardless of gender and teaching experience, most of the teachers believe that the emergence of fear has affected and limited the ways in which they work: "I am always thinking about what I am doing, I'm always aware of the risks" and "I am more on guard now." More on guard indicates that they are aware of the problem and have in some ways changed the way they work.

On the other hand, some teachers do not think that physical contact with the students is a problem in their daily work. They do not experience anxieties like some other teachers do. They instead defend the use of physical contact in a variety of pedagogical situations to do a good job and help the students to achieve the goals stated in the curriculum. Some teachers say that more physical contact is needed in education and one teacher expresses: "It should not be a matter of 'no touching,' but of more touching. Humans need physical touch").

Pedagogically Relevant Physical Contact in PE

Although the teachers express a "constant awareness," they also emphasize the necessity of physical contact in their teaching. They argue that physical contact is important in a variety of educational situations. We have identified three arguments that focus on why physical contact is relevant for students' development and learning.

*Touching as a Precondition for a
Certain Subject Content*

The teachers point to two reasons why physical contact between teacher and students is necessary for particular subject content: some subject content involves the risk of injury, and some subject content requires nonverbal instruction. Physical contact is considered more necessary in relation to some subject content than others. The activities that are primarily mentioned as requiring physical contact are gymnastics, dance, fitness and strength training, ice-skating, swimming (lifesaving) and some collaborative games. In ice-skating it is about helping the students to balance and in gymnastics, physical contact is seen as essential for preventing potential injuries:

> *You must support the students in some risky movements. It is about preventing injuries, and about safety. Some exercises are dangerous, such as somersaults on trampoline, movements using rings or on the bar. It is simply about avoiding neck and back injuries.*

The teachers also argue that they need to use physical contact to guide the students toward a correct movement and in that way physically helping the students to complete the movement, or "get it right" in a corrective sense. The student's body needs to be tangibly brought into the right position with the purpose of creating a physical sense of the movement itself.

> *I usually pat certain parts of the body so that they can feel their bodies and their muscles, keep a check on their arms and legs. I usually ask: Can you feel this? I say that you should feel it here and put my hand on a muscle or on part of the body so they can*

> *feel it. If I only give verbal instructions many don't understand, many students don't know where the muscles are.*

The teachers use physical contact to help the students to develop a sense of and knowledge about their own bodies. In this, the teachers stress the importance of communicating both verbally and nonverbally. If teachers are not allowed to physically touch students, some subject content would have to be omitted (as too risky) and the teaching of some content would be negatively impacted (only verbal instructions allowed).

Instructional touch and physical support are necessary for most students when learning bodily skills. One teacher states: "By spotting and support I can help the students to succeed with an exercise." Physical contact here is necessary for learning certain subject content and thus relevant for students' development.

Touching as a Way of Establishing a Good Relationship

Many teachers talk about the value of warm relationships between students and teachers for learning. The teachers argue that, as educators, any interaction with students involves both a human and a professional encounter. According to them, physical contact contributes to the creation of a personal relationship and a climate of respect and tolerance. Some teachers hold that physical contact is a natural way of communicating, and thus a good way of creating a good relationship.

> *I use physical contact as a way of creating good relations. My way of working is comprised of physical contact to create better learning situations. It is about creating a natural everyday touch—this is how we meet each other.*

But it is not just the teachers who initiate physical contact during the lessons. Most teachers describe how some students want to interact physically with them and indicate this by searching for some form of physical connection.

> *Students seek physical contact. I usually lift them up and hurl them onto the thick carpet. Joke with them when they come and push me. This creates a tighter relationship, creates trust, which in turn creates better teaching situations and learning conditions.*

The teachers also talk about how physical contact can be employed as a positive drive in the learning environment. This can take the form of a tactile congratulation, a hug or a "high five" when a student has overcome a difficult challenge. One teacher says: "I wouldn't be able to do my job if I wasn't allowed to touch the students." A learning environment that allows physical contact is regarded as particularly important, especially in a subject where body and movement are central issues.

Touching as a Human Necessity and as an Expression of Care

The teachers claim that human touch is an essential part of being human. One teacher goes as far as saying, "We wither without physical contact." They also talk about physical contact as a social necessity in our society in which interpersonal relationships are based on mutual respect and exchange. The teachers claim that education has an important role to play in socializing children and young people to embrace tactile touch and physical interaction as a way of being with others.

> *I want to defend the tactile, it's healthy, it creates security. People die without physical contact and relationships. The school has a role to play here. Our subject has all the preconditions for it. Through physical contact we become less afraid of each other. If we touched each other, without coercion, more spontaneously, everyone would feel better. But I am careful about hugging. I'm afraid of how it might be interpreted.*

The teachers further connect physical contact to sympathy and care. Caring for others is seen as a general human responsibility and caring for children is included in the responsibility of the teacher. They talk about how their own convictions of the importance of physical contact for humans sometimes clash with the difficulties surrounding physical contact with students. Although the teachers are worried about the dangers of physical contact in their pedagogical work, they are more worried about the dangers of not touching children.

> *We don't work with machines. Showing affection, meeting someone who doesn't feel well, then a pat on the shoulder is important. Imagine not getting a hug when you are sad! It's about emotions and caring.*

The teachers talk about physical contact as a basic human need that is vital both to the individual student's well-being and to human relations in our society. They also make a strong connection between caring for others and physical contact within the responsibility of education. One teacher says: "I feel like I want to teach them what a positive living touch is all about." The teachers struggle somewhat with this basic conviction but reach the conclusion that physical contact is worth protecting and preserving and is too vital to abandon in educational practice. Indeed, it may even be perceived as "inhuman" to remove physical contact from some caring situations.

Teaching Strategies in Relation to Physical Contact

In relation to the child protection discourse and "no-touch" policy, the teachers' self-regulation is about developing avoidance-oriented strategies or downplaying-oriented strategies. These different strategies are partly about what teachers do with their own bodies, but also what they do or do not do in relation to the students' bodies. They consider how to regulate themselves in relation to where to touch, how to touch, when to touch, and whom to touch.

Avoidance-Oriented Strategies

One of the problems associated with physical contact is the amount and type of clothing worn by students. Activities in which students' clothing is minimal, for example when swimming and in the gym, are particularly risky for teachers in terms of where their gaze falls. Some teachers find it difficult to know where and how to look and describe how careful they are when teaching students. In terms of self-regulation, they avoid looking at the student's bodies and direct their gaze elsewhere:

> *I'm very careful about my gaze. I avoid looking at their bodies and try to look elsewhere. When we have swimming, I mostly look up at the ceiling.*

When it comes to learning situations, teachers are more careful about making physical contact with students who are scantily dressed. One teacher says: "I feel vulnerable, and you have to watch out." The teachers deal with their gaze in different ways and try to look at the students' faces or somewhere above their heads. One teacher has solved the problem by allowing the students to video-record themselves:

> *It's a big dilemma, this gaze. I avoid looking at the students. But it is my job to assess what they are doing. So I have to look at them. Now I ask them to video-record themselves doing a warm-up or a fitness training program so that I can assess and evaluate their movements. I have solved the problem in that way.*

The gaze is less problematic for teachers of outdoor activities such as skiing and skating. It is easier to interact physically when students are wearing tracksuits rather than swimsuits, in that their clothing acts as a barrier.

The fear of being misinterpreted of misbehavior has led teachers to develop different strategies. When it comes to physical contact, some of the teachers say that they never touch the students with open hands but always clench them to avoid possible sexual connotations: "I clench my fist and touch the students with my clenched fist, because a clenched fist cannot be interpreted as a caress."

By saying, "a clenched fist cannot be interpreted as a caress," it is obvious in this case that self-regulation is related to an awareness of situations in which the body has become sexualized. This is also clear when it comes to choosing someone with whom to demonstrate moves or steps. One male teacher says: "I never demonstrate with the best-looking girl in the class." When working with pair exercises, showing gymnastic moves or dancing, most teachers avoid demonstrating with the opposite sex. One male teacher says: "If I'm going to demonstrate something with a student, or if there are odd numbers, I usually join in. But then I always choose a boy. That's just one of the strategies I use."

Both female and male teachers, regardless of their teaching experience, think that it is important to tell students that they will touch them in some of the activities and often do this before or at the beginning of a lesson, so that they have witnesses and the students' permission. Things that were previously considered natural in terms of physical support for certain exercises are now no longer obvious. Many teachers tell the students what to expect, for example in an apparatus gymnastics lesson: "I'm going to stand here at the side and watch because I don't want you to break your neck. If necessary, I'll put my hand on your hip in order to help you over."

The teachers seem to have a fear that physical contact will be interpreted as something sexual. This is clear when the teachers talk about the gaze, a clenched fist and an avoidance of demonstrating with the opposite sex.

Downplaying-Oriented Strategies

Downplaying is partly about defusing a situation in which physical contact is used. Here, teachers try to avoid being affected by the child protection discourse and "no-touch" policy and instead emphasize physical contact as something necessary and natural in PE. Self-regulation is thus about playing down physical contact and seeing it as a natural part of the subject.

Several teachers believe that the body has become sexualized in our society, and therefore it is important to highlight other perspectives on the body. In many respects, it is a matter to de-dramatize the body as a sexual object by acting as though physical contact is the most natural thing in the world. An older female teacher says: "I'm already 'desexualized,'" and her strategy is to try to defuse the issue. For example, when students are wrestling or boxing and need to be physically close to each other, she says: "I know you guys think about sex, but this is actually boxing/wrestling. Physical contact goes with the subject."

In gymnastics, teachers must support and help students with exercises, and in this, different parts of the body are touched. All the teachers are aware that sensitive situations can arise when supporting students in some of the gymnastic activities and have devised strategies to deal with this. A strategy they use is to tell students outright that there will be physical contact during the lesson, act as though nothing is wrong, and physical contact is no big deal. One teacher says that he accidentally touched a girl's breast whilst helping her to do a somersault on a mini trampoline. Although anxious about what might happen next, he decided not to say anything but simply acted as though it was the most natural thing in the world. Several of the teachers do not say anything about physical contact during the lesson, because they believe that students will become more preoccupied and suspicious about it:

> *If I happen to touch a person's thigh when I am supporting them, and have talked about this before, they might get suspicious.*

Some teachers try to teach children physical contact right from the start and regard it as part of the profession, part of the subject and as supporting learning. Already in infant classes some teachers adopt the approach that physical contact is natural:

> *As I said, defusing the issue is important. I work a lot with drive-car exercises among the children. One of them is the driver and*

the other is a car. The car must shut its eyes. They have to touch and trust each other.

In this theme, self-regulation is largely to do with downplaying-oriented strategies. The teachers try to defuse physical contact by showing that it is not about sexuality but is instead a natural and important part of the subject content. They choose not to make a big deal about it, use humor and teach children about physical contact from the start. They are aware of the complexity and the need for fingertip sensitivity.

Physical Education Teachers' Professionalism

This part of the chapter regards a crucial question about if and how the Child protection discourse, the international influence of no-touch policy documents and the teachers concern about physical contact may affect teachers' professional identity.

The selected illustrations in the chapter show a complex, and quite problematic, picture regarding physical contact between teacher and student in teaching practice. The complexity is, on the one hand, that the teachers emphasize the great pedagogical value of physical interaction, and that physical contact seems to be both relevant and necessary as an integral component of students' development, learning, and growth. On the other hand, many teachers have a concern, an uncertainty about how to physically meet the students. The greatest fear lies in being accused of sexual harassment and the teachers have developed different strategies for handling physical contact—avoidance- or downplaying-oriented strategies.

We believe that some changes are gradually taking place in the school subject Physical Education. The once stable and relatively autonomous position of the PE teaching profession has been called into question. These changes will in one way or another affect the content of the subject, student learning and not least the teachers' professional identity. Of course, changes always happen in school and changes do not necessarily have to be negative. But, we want to draw attention to what seems to be happening to teachers' professional identity because of the anxiety and uncertainty that seems to follow the "touching or no-touch" issue in teaching situations.

As an educator, any interaction with students involves both a human and a professional encounter, which means that you as a teacher meet the student in the role of a fellow human being and in the role of an educator with specific objectives. However, in a culture in which teachers are afraid of making mistakes, afraid of being misinterpreted when supporting a handstand, it becomes difficult to maintain professional pride. If PE practice becomes a "no-touch zone" and teachers always avoid touching the children (an approach that the student teachers indicated in the story at the introduction of the book had clearly absorbed) may result in many of the teachers' pedagogical tools being weakened. In PE, where body and movement are central, it is important to ask whether it is possible to learn about the body's potential and body movements by verbal communication alone. However, it is not just about physical abilities; it is also about the general goals of education in terms of developing students' personalities, their capacity for empathy, and social and moral shaping.

We think that certain learning situations will be hard to deal with in an effective way. The risk could be that teachers will find it difficult to develop students' motor skills and physical abilities, to prevent injuries and deal with "risky" situations, to cope with social situations involving behaviors and manners and to spontaneously express caring and joy.

Things that were previously considered natural in terms of physical support for certain exercises are now no longer obvious.

Established habits and pedagogical solutions have been developed by the teaching staff for a long time. Fears and uncertainty obviously affect these habits and solutions. We do not know the long-term consequences of how different touch- and self-regulations affect the professional identity. To strengthen the somewhat corroded teacher professionalism, it is important to ask questions about how historical traditions, ideologies (see Chapter 4), and the core of professional identity have been challenged and even transformed.

We believe that both the pedagogy and teachers' professional identity are under threat, due to the culture of fear and uncertainty amongst teachers. They are now under pressure to show appropriate behaviour regarding physical contact and avoid problematic incidents. That kind of pressure has in many ways resulted in a paralyzing and defensive practice. Having to constantly ask yourself about appropriate or inappropriate touch in your everyday work creates confusion about your own professional identity and the profession. In a way, professionals can now be said to work from a culture of anxiousness instead of caring and the professional use of physical contact in PE has come to be viewed as malpractice rather than pedagogy.

Questions to Discuss

- Did your teachers or coaches discuss physical contact in learning situations? Have they discussed physical contact in the hands-on activity you have participated in?
- How would you, as a teacher or coach, handle and talk about physical contact in the activity that you engage in?
- What implications can the different strategies developed by the teachers have for children's and young people's physical capabilities, learning and development?

CHAPTER 4

Physical Contact and Teaching Techniques[1]

In the introduction, we expressed concerns about the critical aspects of physical contact in teaching and coaching, and how our embodied basis for engaging in the physical education (PE) profession had changed. In chapter three, we explained and discussed teachers' strategies by emphasizing self-governing processes and the ways in which PE teachers regulate themselves in relation to the no-touch discourse (Jones, 2004; Öhman, 2017). In this chapter, we will describe and explain why PE teachers use techniques of physical contact. Because, despite the no-touch discourse and many complex issues surrounding physical contact it remains a significant educational tool. Teachers give instructions, practice caring support and build durable relationships with pupils and athletes. Many such actions include physical contact as an educational tool, for example holding on to an arm while showing a movement or just patting a shoulder to express care. When teachers refrain from physical contact, they therefore refrain also from some of their embodied habits on which their practical knowledge of teaching is grounded. At the same time, it is an evident risk to use physical contact because they can be accused of sexual harassment. This means that teachers must strike a balance between the risks of using physical contact and the risks of ultimately refraining from physical contact. The risk of refraining from physical contact is that they will lose some of their instructional techniques and habits of caring for students/athletes. In this way, those who use physical contact, either as an instructional aid or simply by wiping a tear, will have to live with the following conflict: do I challenge no-touch policies in order to care for my students and athletes, or do I challenge my student and athlete relationships in order to care for the no-touch policies? If teachers care too much for their students, they may fail to care adequately for themselves and disable themselves as caregivers. However, if teachers care too much for themselves, they may fail to adequately care for their students and thereby fail to adequately answer their *call to teach*. Paradoxes such as these highlight teaching as a caring profession and is what we in this chapter refer to as the essential tension of touching in teaching physical education. A call to teach means that the best interests of the pupils or athletes become the interests of the teacher or sports pedagogue.

In using the concepts of body pedagogic and care, we now move from physical contact as a discursive and power-related problem, to rather understand it as embodied teaching techniques through which teachers handle caring relationships at different levels. The concepts of body pedagogics and care thereby opens for an understanding of PE teachers' profession as a shared cultural knowledge about how to navigate intimacy in teaching. In the following, we, therefore, first present body pedagogy as a specific approach to the phenomenon of physical contact. We then explain the essential tension of physical contact in physical education and thereafter describe three different techniques of physical contact that answer teachers' call to teach. Through these three techniques we highlight how and when techniques of physical contact are used, what teaching intention that can be connected to these techniques, and what is the potential tension in these techniques.

Body Pedagogics and Techniques of Physical Contact

Given the last decades of developments explained in the introduction the learning environments of schools have been transformed. This transformation of the learning environment has consequences at a very concrete level for teachers' and coaches' experiences, professional skills, and embodied habits. To explain these consequences the main perspective has often been to view the body as a location for social structure. That is, how no-touch policies form the context for embodied action and shape teaching habits, values, and norms (Öhman, 2017). For example, how teachers have come to alter their instruction techniques by touching students with a clenched fist, or only using verbal instructions when guiding complex movements. The benefit of the perspective of the body as a location for social structure is that research has successfully challenged us to think critically about no-touch policies, for instance, in considering whether alterations of teaching techniques in order to adopt no-touch policies are successful for students' and athletes' learning (e.g., Piper, 2015b; Piper et al., 2012; Taylor et al., 2016). However, in this chapter, we argue for an approach that understands physical contact as deeply associated with specific teaching techniques and hence as an intrinsic part of a call to teach.

The body sociologist Chris Shilling's concept of body pedagogy (2007, 2008, 2022) concerns the relationship between the social, technological, and material means through which a practice like teaching is transmitted. In this process, teachers and students make many different experiences that also result in outcomes such as different habits and techniques. Through the lens of body pedagogy, we can focus on how PE teachers and sports pedagogues on an everyday basis use numerous techniques that involve physical contact. Furthermore, we can describe how these are connected to specific traditional purposes such as guidance, encouragement, and safety. Guidance could here mean pointing out which muscles to use, or correct posture, while encouragement could be a pat on the back or a high five, and safety is about techniques that prevent children from being injured. The body pedagogy approach of this chapter thereby gives us a starting point where we position PE teachers as reflective practitioners capable of handling the essential tension of touching. That essential tension is represented by the question, Do I challenge no-touch policies in order to care for my students, or do I challenge my student relationships in order to care for the no-touch policies? Reflections and knowledge about if, how, when, and whom to touch in educational settings have, in this way, always been an important part of PE teachers' and sports pedagogues' profession, even long before the occurrence of no-touch policies and the public debate around intergenerational touch. The reason we explain techniques of physical contact as skillful teacher actions is that we find it important to recognize teachers', and also other sports pedagogues', professionalism, that is, their competence in handling essential tensions and ethical dilemmas in everyday teaching. Thus, through a body pedagogy approach the challenge is not to argue intellectually about the pros and cons of physical contact but to analyze how teachers handle student encounters and teaching intentions. We, therefore, focus on teachers' ways of interacting with students through different techniques of physical contact. Instead of explaining how bodies are governed by discursive power, which means teaching techniques are altered and the use of physical contact very restrictive because of the no-touch policies, we approach issues around no-touch policies as a practical teacher concern. As a practical teacher concern, no-touch policies are always weighted by teachers in relation to already established professional habits and values that assist their call to teach.

Embodied Teaching Values

Research has long argued that a caring teacher–student relationship provides teachers and sports pedagogues with the foundations on which they can undertake the social and moral shaping of future citizens (McCuaig et al., 2013; Miller, 2012; Owens & Ennis, 2005). Teachers engage in their chosen practice because they care about specific values and the good of helping others share them (Piper, 2015b). Several studies show that core values of pedagogic professions are bodily grounded in its praxis and constitution of a call to teach. But few empirical studies connect bodily grounded values to what we in this chapter explain as techniques of physical contact. Important for our approach are, for example, Lyons' (2014, p. 146) optimistic account of teaching and coaching habits; McWilliam and Jones (2005), who discuss the relation between child welfare and professional integrity; and Steckley (2012), who emphasizes on professional practice instead of strong regulations of caring acts. In using various techniques of physical contact, teachers must manage their call to teach according to challenges related to physical contact. It is only by thoroughly depicting the experiences and techniques of everyday practitioners that practitioners as well as researchers can understand whether a certain discourse is reproduced (see chap three), and whether certain teaching techniques have their expected outcomes. Again, what we are dealing with here is the essential tension of teaching and physical contact.

To describe how different techniques of physical contact include different and essential tensions which the teachers constantly reflect on, we discuss teachers' views about how they use bodily touch in their interaction with students in different situations. These techniques are established and practiced by teachers for specific purposes. Security touch is a technique that pedagogues use to prevent injuries, denotative touch is used when pointing out specific qualities of movements, and relational touch is about creating relationships and comfort in learning environments. Our identification of these three techniques draws on interviews with PE teachers in Swedish primary, secondary, and upper-secondary schools. Before we describe and explain them more in detail. We have to more thoroughly ground our perspective of teaching as a caring profession.

Teaching as a Caring Profession

With inspiration from the educational philosopher Jim Garrison and his book, *Dewey and Eros: Wisdom and desire in the art of teaching* (2010), three different dimensions are crucial here to help us understand the complexity of using physical contact in pedagogic situations. These dimensions are: (i) the ambiguity of teaching intention where we explain the variability of how physical contact can be interpreted, (ii) ethics of care and ethics of justice which point to the fact that teachers must balance between different logic of ethics when encountering students, and (iii) the paradox of caring that describes the ultimate choices that teachers sometimes must make about saving themselves or saving the very mission of teaching. Together, these three dimensions help us to understand physical contact not only as a discursive and power-related question but also as an essential tension that always accompanies teaching and that prompts practical wisdom (Garrison, 2010).

The Ambiguity of Teaching Intention

One of the problems of using techniques of physical contact in pedagogical practices is that we cannot determine the intention of such touching simply by looking at it. The teachers' purposes that guide an educational act of physical contact are not self-interpreting. The same action can be subject to a potentially endless array of interpretations. The same act of touching may be interpreted one way by the teacher, another way by the student touched, a different way by other students that witnessed the act, and yet another way by an educational administrator or even a judge in a courtroom. Human intentions have an ambiguity that teachers and sports pedagogues must learn to live with when using techniques of bodily touch. That ambiguity is part of the essential tension of physical contact in physical education as well as in other sports-related pedagogical contexts. Caring, as a practical pedagogical concern, therefore requires wisdom regarding the right time to use physical contact and to refrain from such use. This wisdom involves the ability to discern students' needs, to understand what they desire, to meet their interests and purposes in particular situations and act appropriately. This requires good common sense most often acquired only through extensive practice.

Ethics of Care and Ethics of Justice

An ethics of care has to do with emotional responses within personal relations and contextualized situations. It tends to dominate in private spaces such as friendship, family, teacher–student relationships, and team sports. This is visible when teachers engage in creating sound relationships and invite students to take part in activities not merely as motor skill learners but as personal selves and fellow practitioners. In this way, the educational philosopher Jim Garrison relates teachers' ethics of care to a practical wisdom and distinguishes it from empathy. While empathy assumes students are like us and that "we may project our need and desires upon them" (Garrison, 2010), ethics of care is more of a moral conviction that "possesses the poetic power to actualize the good in everyday affairs" (Garrison, 2010). As PE teachers, we do not have the artistic freedom to practice our poetic power at all times but must ground our practice in laws and regulations too. An ethics of justice emphasizes such decontextualized abstract rules, laws, regulations, and rights ordered in a fixed hierarchy. Ethics of justice, furthermore, emphasizes dispassionate calculation as for example when we think of justice as "blind" and "impartial." It also includes abstract rules and regulations of policy that dominate legal systems and institutions such as school and sports clubs. In this way, ethics of justice governs the caring profession of teaching and as practicing teachers we will have to submit in some way or another to ethics of justice. When our rules come into conflict, rules higher on the hierarchy often supersede those that are lower. We will therefore always have to balance an ethics of justice with an ethics of care that is grounded in our call to teach. One way to illustrate that essential tension is to state the conflict as the way we did in the introduction of the chapter: Do I compromise the rules (ethics of justice) to save my students (ethics of care), or compromise my students (ethics of care), to save the rules (ethics of justice)?

The Paradox of Caring

The call to teach means that the best interests of the students become the interests of the teacher. The caregiver (i.e., teacher or sports pedagogue) must act, but the caregiver alone cannot decide if the act of caring is adequate and complete. The cared-for (the student or athlete) must show some sign of recognition. Whether the teaching act of physical contact will play out in the way the teacher planned depends on the teacher's ability to reach an educational purpose that responds to his or her intention to use physical contact. To reach such a purpose is a collective commitment between the teacher and students (what we in chap 5 relate to as "the didactic contract"). When teachers express care, they are both self-serving and other serving. The paradox of caring, in practice, is that it is rarely good for teachers to reduce their capacity to care for students by failing to care for themselves (Garrison, 2010). We may state the paradox of caring regarding techniques of physical contact in PE as follows: For those PE teachers that answer their call to teach, it is sometimes necessary to care for their students by touching them; however, to care well for their students, they must also care for themselves by sometimes refraining from touching. Should they care too much for themselves, they may fail to adequately care for their students, or, ironically enough, fail to answer their call to teach. Given the public debate regarding physical contact and heightened concerns for children's welfare in recent years (see chaps 1 and 2), it is understandable that many teachers may choose to care for themselves instead of their students. For example, by simply not touching at all or touching in clumsy or awkward ways such as with a clenched fist (Öhman, 2016).

Teachers that use techniques of physical contact must learn to live with the paradox of caring. It is part of the essential tension of physical contact in pedagogical practices.

We will now use the three different dimensions of teaching as a caring profession to describe the details of how three different techniques of physical contact include care and different tensions. Our descriptions rely on one of our research projects where we interviewed teacher educators about their first-hand experiences of encounters with students that resulted in certain tensions for them.

Three Different Techniques of Physical Contact

As noted in the introduction, teachers must balance between adaptations to public no-touch discourses and carrying out a personal call to teach. Theoretically, that balance can be explained by understanding teaching as a caring profession that includes (i) the ambiguity of teaching intention, (ii) ethics of care and ethics of justice, and (iii) the paradox of teaching. Based on that understanding, and that PE teachers' body pedagogy must handle interactions with students in relation to physical contact, we describe and discuss three different techniques of physical contact and the purposes for which these are used. In doing so, we point out PE teachers' competence in handling different functions of physical contact while teaching. To understand the techniques of physical contact, we see them as a part of an educational context where PE teachers must learn to live wisely with the tensions while recognizing the inevitable social barriers to securing the goods of their practice. That is, techniques of physical contact rely on professional skills as well as certain values and norms, which are established and practiced with specific purposes for safety, guidance, and encouragement. We have named these techniques (i) security touch, (ii) denotative touch, and (iii) relational touch. Each of the techniques relies on professional assessments whether it meets its intended purpose and are important for teachers in carrying out their call to teach. Indeed, it is possible for the same teaching act to be connected to all three techniques, or another technique that we may have failed to identify in our research. To point out important details when describing the techniques of physical contact will pose the following questions to each technique: (i) How and when do teachers use this technique of physical contact? (ii) What teaching intention can be connected to this technique? (iii) What is the potential tension in this technique?

Physical Contact and Teaching Techniques

Security Touch

Security touch is used when teachers try to identify or prevent injuries and deal with high-risk situations by supporting movements. For example, when students carry out complex physical activities. They also use physical contact to assess injuries if the students have already hurt themselves. In this way, security touch is characterized by intentions to handle the fragile student body. By feeling and touching, wiggling a foot in different ways and asking, "What does it feel like?" teachers try to find out what and where the injury is and what might have caused it. In teachers' descriptions about situations like these, it is often visible that the teacher and the student simultaneously use bodily resources for identifying a problem. Thereby, they work with the body collectively in a specific direction.

When teaching in apparatus gymnastics teachers are compelled to secure safe practice for the students. Here, physical contact is a security tool that is necessary to let the student participate in gymnastic activity. However, even when physical contact is inevitable due to security reasons, there is a potential tension present. One of the teachers we interviewed told us that when he supported a student doing somersaults on a mini trampoline, he accidentally touched the girl's breast when he tried to stop her flying off the mat. She got up and looked at a friend as if to say, "Did you see that?" But then she went back and did the exercise two minutes later again, and nothing else happened. Despite this, the teacher could not help but wonder, "What will happen now?" Such immediate feelings about moments when physical contact becomes awkward are very common for PE teachers. Knowledge about how to read the cues, physically as well as ethically, is substantial in assessing the educative meaning of security touch. In addition, it is very clear the teacher's vulnerability is increased in the caring act of security touch. When the student comes back for a second try the teacher can weigh and judge if the embodied intention of a security touch is received, or if he must use another technique to meet the student's needs and desires. This example illustrates how complicated it is to entirely eliminate the ambiguity of teaching intentions. Moreover, it is noticeable how teachers try to handle this ambiguity in relation to a specific technique of security touch. It is not "touch" in itself that is the object of reflection for the teacher here; he/she does not think: Do I have to stop touching my students? Rather, he/she is forced to consider their embodied teaching tool in relation to the student. This continuous awareness of making security touch appropriate and educationally purposeful is also brought to the fore in the different choices teachers give students. The teacher ensures that by saying to the student, "I'll stand here, and I'll support you, if you don't want me to support you then you'll just have to do ordinary straight jumps on the trampoline over there and that's OK." At the same time, they do not let the student take the full responsibility and get hurt if they refrain from physical touch; teachers must make sure that "if something gets completely wrong, I'll come and hold you." In the teachers' explanations of how they work with security touch, they emphasize the necessity of safety to contextualize bodily touch and relate it to a particular purpose. If students do something "completely wrong" or are about to "fall" the teacher will always be their safety net. Whether a technique of bodily touch will have this intended outcome is dependent on the teacher reaching an educational purpose that responds to this intention. Even security touch, which might be understood as an ethics of justice, is subject to the vicissitudes of its embodied intention. Teachers express a need to be receptive to students' needs and desires (e.g., how they respond when a teacher accidently touches a breast), to ensure that the meaning of physical contact is established as security touch rather than as just inappropriate physical contact.

Denotative Touch

Denotative touch is characterized by intentions to handle learning content. Teachers use denotative touch to convey the desired body movement, thus helping students attend to certain qualities in order to develop different motor skills. It is about bringing the body into the right position to create a sense of the movement itself. Teachers explain, for example, that in athletics you have to go in and get hold of the arm, "Can you feel what that movement feels like, and that movement?" or when doing the shot put in track and field they have to instruct and point out learning content in action by using denotative touch, "This is where the shot should be, both shoulders, that should be there and that should rest" and so on. This frequent use of denotative touch to point out muscles and movements in action is also common in teaching dance, for example with the Jive, where teachers tell that "there's a lot of for example strengthening the right leg, left shoulder." In our interview with PE teachers, we have also noted that they use denotative touch to help students distinguish among feelings, "What does that movement feel like?" "There, there, right." Such help from teachers help the student develop a selective attention for a body part or body parts in relation to a posture, and learn where to feel a consequence of a certain movement, which very often relies on denotative touch. All these examples illustrate how teachers struggle to teach students to correctly intuit certain qualities of movements. In such a context, verbal instruction or the use of metaphors will not always do the job and the teacher can use denotative touch. For example, when a teacher helps a student with doing a pike shape by holding the student's legs and creating a feeling of a certain quality of a posture, "Here, you should be here." It often requires a similar instruction when teaching muscle training and getting the exercise as right and effective as possible. Here, at some levels, the students do not have the ability to distinguish the critical position of, say, a shoulder. Then, an easy tap on the shoulder helps the teacher to create a focus and direct learning. However, such distinct and direct physical contact must be conceived as part of teachers and students working together with the technique of denotative touch. That is, they must agree on a joint purpose of why they are doing it the way they do. When students, for example, work with dumbbells, the teacher can press on the back when students are lifting, asking, "Can you feel how tense the muscles are now?" If there is no tension, they can ask students to change the movement while keeping the hand on the back and tell them when the muscle tensions. In this way, it is possible for the teacher to point out how dumbbells stretch muscles and not the arm. By having students attend to a specific muscle, and ignore another muscle of part of the body, denotative touch also helps students to point out "tense" and "not tense" as crucial qualities. The teachers further explain that it is crucial students make experiences of what it feels like in the body when it is done right. Physical contact in this context is directed toward making the students feel their own body, not the teacher's body. In this molding of the body, to get students to notice crucial consequences of the exercise, it is important that the cared-for (students) show some sign of recognition. The teacher alone cannot decide if the act of caring is adequate and complete. The moment a student feels the teacher's body, instead of the quality that the teacher points to in the exercise, the embodied intention of denotative touch would most probably misfire and there is no joint purpose between the teacher and the student.

Denotative touch can also be used in order to fulfil a movement together with the student. For example, when students try to jump up in the rings and hang upside down, they often need that little extra push on the back or the bottom in order to get up there. And if they get that final push, they will soon find a way of doing it themselves. In situations such as these denotative touch is used to make overlapping movements toward a specific end, to fulfil the tactile experience of "getting up." In these situations, teachers can feel limited by verbal instructions, and they must simply follow through on the movement together with the student. In so doing, the teacher helps the student to achieve a closure of a particular movement. However, it is not for the teacher to decide whether it is a closure of the teaching intention to give a student an experience of "getting up." To be able to use a technique of physical contact in specific teaching contexts requires continuous professional assessments about whether physical contact meets its intended purpose and has the function of a denotative touch. When a teacher uses denotative touch and a student responds to its embodied intention, the interests of the other (student) becomes the interests of the one-caring (the teacher), that is, the technique of physical contact becomes a constitutive part of the teacher's call to teach. Likewise, if another student in a similar situation refrains from denotative touch, the teacher must be able to use another technique to meet the student's needs. To insist on a single teaching technique at all times will never make it a constitutive part of the teacher's call to teach.

Relational Touch

Security and denotative touch are very subject specific in their teaching content. The students should learn how to control their movements without hurting themselves and be able to feel their own bodies. Relational touch is more explicitly characterized by broader caring intentions and is not used to direct subject-specific content. Using relational touch, the teachers try to create good relationships and atmosphere, express joy and communicate their own feelings (see also Öhman & Quennerstedt, 2017). Furthermore, relational touch is used to create a private space, to individualize teaching and caring as well as include and recognize students' experiences of a lesson or a practice. This means that what characterizes relational touch is that teachers aim for something essential that goes beyond mere subject-specific content. This is evident in how teachers sit down to share a private space with students, for example, by putting a hand on a knee and just showing, "now I'm here, now I'm talking to you." Teachers also express their desire to comfort or in some ways calm the students down to make them understand that "there's just you and me, I'm talking to you the others aren't there." The use of relational touch in these and similar situations reveal teachers' intention to encounter students as living persons and is a teaching act clearly connected to the ambiguity of teaching intentions. If teachers chose to use physical contact with such caring intentions, they truly must balance between a care and ethics justice. Again, the important practical question is what this technique of relational touch would require to work according to its purpose? If the students shun the teacher's caring act and yet the teacher uses the technique, it will ruin the trust between student and teacher. However, from a teacher perspective relational touch is not merely about performing or refraining from performing an intentional teaching act. For caring to be maintained, the one-caring must be maintained. This maintenance of a call to teach is seen in teachers' reasoning about how many communications they have during a day. They use quick communications all the time such as, "Hi, how are you? Fine, just fine, hi, why don't you have any kit with you today? OK, so you've got a pain in your knee. Yes, we'll fix it later." In these quick communications, they mostly just want a quick response. But there is also a described urge to meet the students on a deeper and more meaningful level than is possible in the everyday teaching activity where students and classes come and go. To meet the student on this level, the teacher must use a technique that answers their call to teach. The teachers describe that they worry about not being able to notice students during lessons and make up for this, for example, by walking with them toward the locker room and just patting them on the shoulders and saying, "Well done today." This helps teachers to acknowledge the students. If the teacher feels he/she has not been able to share a particular learning moment together with certain students, they use bodily touch to express, "I've seen you but that I've been busy." To handle such teaching experience, relational touch is used to express directly to the students that they are an important part of their teaching. In contrast to just standing 3 m away and shouting, "Well done" the teachers believe in a more trustful relationship when, for example, a walk-along touch is included. In this way, teachers' intentions of relational touch are to help the students feel teacher acknowledgment of a certain participation or performance. When talking to teachers about their use of relational touch, the paradox of caring is really brought to the fore. On the one hand, these relational intentions can seem to bring forward good empathetic values of teaching. On the other hand, Garrison (2010) reminds us of being wary of empathy as a pedagogical value, because empathy assumes students and athletes are like us and that "we may project our need and desires upon them." This is why Garrison in his statement of teaching as a caring profession make clear that caring means a potentially increased vulnerability. When we care we can be hurt through the other as well as through ourselves. Indeed, the paradox of teaching is evident for those teachers that answer their call to teach by using a technique of relational touch. They can care for their students by using relational touch. At the same time, they care for themselves by an active choice of not using relational touch. Their potentially increased vulnerability is represented, in our examples of physical contact, not necessarily by being accused of sexual harassment or losing the job but rather by the risk of losing an embodied teaching tool and all the professional meanings it binds. This means, that to care for one-selves, also means to care for one's embodied teaching techniques such as security, denotative, and relational touch.

Summary

What we have discussed and illustrated in this chapter is that it is important to not only understand physical contact as a discursive and power-related question. Although such perspectives help explain how teachers, and other sports pedagogues, regulate their use of physical contact in relation to public debate, it is still a description of how society instills certain values into the professional practices. But physical contact is also related to teachers' and sports pedagogues' embodied teaching techniques, and we must therefore recognize their call to teach as a guiding principle of how they navigate essential tensions of physical contact. Embodied teaching techniques are fundamental to how pedagogic professions answer their call to teach and establish a daily work that focuses on meaningful teaching and learning. We have here described a collection of details that support this work and pointed out three different techniques of physical contact that are established and practiced by teachers for specific purposes.

These techniques can be used to understand different pedagogical practices and teachers' habits. Security touch describes intentions to handle the fragile student body, denotative touch describes teachers' intentions to handle learning content and helping the students attend to certain qualities to develop different skills, and relational touch describes teachers' caring intentions and how they handle relationships and recognize students' experiences.

The body pedagogy approach (Shilling, 2007) we employed in this chapter further challenges researchers and practitioners to never stop exploring whether techniques of physical contact achieve desired educational outcomes or simply reproduce mainstream culture around child protection within schools. It is a rather strong claim to say that if traditional techniques of physical contact disappear from practice, PE teaching as a caring profession would cease to exist. However, what we do insist on is that we must handle questions about what teaching, as a caring profession, must regain if the techniques disappear. Our identified techniques of physical contact rely on the teachers' invitations to the students to participate in acts involving physical contact. In relation to security touch this is seen in teacher and student's use of bodily resources to identify pain, as well as having another go on the mat despite an accidental touch of a breast. In relation to denotative touch, it is seen in how the teacher leads the students to feeling their own muscles as tense and soft as well as overlapping movements to come to closure in a certain movement. In relation to relational touch, it is seen in the creation of personal space to be able to create dialogue, or, responding on a shoulder tap for good work. If the PE teachers did not experience any essential tension, the techniques would have long since disappeared. The tension requires PE teachers to function as reflective practitioners in realizing their call to teach.

It is impossible to secure absolute certainty about each teacher's actual intentions in making their statements about physical contact. Although we can never be certain about the intentions of other teachers, we can still make descriptions of how they seek to reach educational purposes by using techniques of physical contact. Whether a teaching act will realize its embodied intention depends on the teacher's ability to reach an educational purpose that responds to this intention. In an era of no-touch policies, some techniques of physical contact may not necessarily be at risk because they fulfil purposes compatible with a non-touching policy, for example, ethics of justice. When relational touch is practiced under the control of an ethics of justice, the technique, as such, is sustainable. However, its embodied intention and teaching purpose have changed in a way that alters the conditions for good teaching practice. It is a major challenge for research to study how teachers, and other sports pedagogues, must dwell wisely at the intersection between adjusting to public discourse and carrying out a personal/professional call to teach.

Questions to Discuss

- What could be examples of when security touch, denotative touch, or relational touch can misfire and there is no joint purpose between teachers and students?
- What would security touch, denotative touch, and relational touch require to work according to its purpose?
- How can sports pedagogues and teachers work to make students feel their own body instead of the teacher's body when using techniques of physical contact?
- What must PE teaching, as a caring profession, regain if the techniques of physical contact disappear?

CHAPTER 5

Physical Contact and Student Reflexivity[1]

In this chapter, students' perspectives of physical contact in physical education (PE) teaching will be discussed. As presented in previous chapters, the student perspective on the issue of physical contact has not been prevalent in research. Rather, research in this field has previously leaned heavily on teachers' perspectives. However, in a school context, students, teachers, and subject content are all integral parts of the teaching and learning. Physical contact is something that emerges in the intersection where these three nodes meet. That is why the student perspective on physical contact also is important. We already know about teachers' fears of being mistrusted or accused of sexual harassment when using physical contact in their teaching. Now, we explore the same in respect of students: How do school students experience physical contact in teaching situations, and do students share teachers' fears and anxieties?

To illustrate students' perspectives, we will utilize data from a study in which two different groups of students in Sweden were interviewed on the topic. The first group of students were Swedish students (born in Sweden with Swedish parents). The other group of students lived in Sweden but had an immigrant background (not born in Sweden). The students were interviewed in groups or pairs, or individually. In all the interviews, photo elicitation was used as an interview technique. The main idea in photo elicitation is to use photographs in the interview situation and ask the participants to comment on them (Bignante, 2010). The photos selected for the interviews depicted PE teachers using physical contact as a pedagogical tool. These included photos of physical contact as a precondition for certain subject content, for example a teacher holding a student's leg in a swimming pool to help the student with breaststroke leg kicks. Photos also related situations where physical contact was used as a way of creating beneficial conditions for learning, such as a teacher giving a student a high five. Lastly, the situations in the photos included physical contact as a human necessity, for instance, a teacher comforting an upset student. The interviews all began with the interviewer laying out the photos (15 different photos) on a table in front of the participants and asking them to describe what they saw in them.

The Didactic Contract

In the didactic tradition, the research focus is mainly on teaching, learning, and subject content and the relations between them. Common research topics in the tradition are what is taught and learned, how it is taught and learned, why it is taught and learned and by whom it is taught and learned (Amade-Escot, 2006; Gundem, 2011; Quennerstedt & Larsson, 2015). Didactical research is often related to the didactic triangle, in which the teacher, student, and subject content are situated at the nodes of a triangle to demonstrate the relations between them. Within the didactical tradition, it is specifically the didactic contract that is of interest in this chapter. The didactic contract is used as an analytical tool to help us understand the relationship between teachers, students, and physical contact. Coined by Brousseau in the 1980s, the didactic contract has been used in educational research in several subjects (Brousseau, 1997; Sarrazy & Novotná, 2013; Verscheure & Amade-Escot, 2007). The didactic contract can be compared to an agreement between teachers and students in which both parties know what to expect from each other in a teaching situation. For example, teachers are expected to create relevant learning conditions for students, while students are expected to live up to these given expectations: "These (specific) habits of the teacher are expected by the student and the behaviour of the students is expected by the teacher; this is the didactical contract" (Brousseau, 1997, p. 225).

Amade-Escot (2017) refers to the didactic contract as a common agreement between teachers and students on the subject content at stake. The agreement or contract is, however, not a formal document or even something spelled out; rather, it is implicitly understood. The rules of such a contract cannot be written or anticipated in advance (Brousseau, 1997), because it is not until the contract is broken or breached that the rules or boundaries of the contract are made visible. The didactic contract is in other words unwritten and can be said to be the result of implicit negotiations between teachers and students about knowledge that is taught in a given situation (Amade-Escot, 2000). One such implicit negotiation can be that students raise their hands if they want to answer a question in class, another is that teachers are expected to share the aims and purposes of the activities chosen for the lessons. If these expectations are not met, they risk breaching the didactic contract. If, for example, a student shouts out an answer in class instead of raising his/her hand, which would be an expected action by the teacher and the other students, this would risk breaching the implicit didactic contract concerning a taken-for-granted norm/rule in many classrooms. Developing abilities in PE is also related to students' understanding and learning of implicit rules and norms that exist in the PE classroom.

Understanding and acting in accordance with these implicit rules and norms can thus be said to be part of the didactic contract. In the context of students' perspectives on physical contact in PE, it is found that when students and teachers agree on when, how, or why physical contact is used, this agreement is part of the process of developing a didactic contract. That is, an implicit agreement between teacher and student concerning physical contact in PE. Breaches of the contract occur if physical contact is used in situations that students do not implicitly or otherwise agree on or expect from the teacher. This means that if a student does not expect physical contact from a teacher but receives it anyway, the physical contact could be perceived as odd or strange. In such a situation, the physical contact would risk breaching the didactic contract about physical contact.

Physical Contact – A Matter of Negotiations

It is clear from the student interviews that physical contact in PE is purpose bound. Simply put, this means that when physical contact has a good purpose it is seen as OK by students. When the teacher and the student agree, or at least know what to implicitly expect from one and other, concerning when, how, and why physical contact is used in the teaching situations, a didactic contract can be said to have been developed between them. It is also evident in the interviews that students decode and negotiate physical contact in different ways, depending on for example what relationship they have developed with teachers. These negotiation aspects also influence the development of an implicit didactic contract or agreement regarding physical contact.

In this section, we present five different themes, which all show different negotiation aspects that the students take into consideration when it comes to the use of physical contact. These aspects (themes) are different ways in which the students negotiate if physical contact from the teacher is legitimate and OK according to them—if it is something that they expect or not in different situations. As a teacher, it is important to be able to have knowledge about how students negotiate physical contact, since it often is used as a pedagogical tool in teaching. The negotiation aspects found in the study referenced here are: (i) teacher professionalism, (ii) practical learning, (iii) teacher empathic skills, (iv) teacher–student relationship, and (v) opposite sex.

i) Teacher Professionalism

The teacher is often referred to in the interviews about physical contact and students indicate that they have faith and trust in the teacher position and profession. They say that physical contact is used because the teachers are simply acting in accordance with their employment and doing their job. One student exemplifies this by saying: "a teacher's job is to get the student to learn something, for that the teacher has to help […] I mean, the teacher is just trying to help" (male student). Trust in the teacher profession is also expressed in terms of the institutional framework where teachers and students act and work. There are in other words rules and regulations that everyone is expected to follow within this framework and professional teachers are expected to follow these rules and do their job.

Part of the teachers' professionalism is in addition their ability to interpret their students' body language and facial expression. The teacher often knows his/her students well enough to be able to tell how they feel by just looking at them (the way they stand, sit, the position of their head, facial expressions), and adjust their way of interacting with them accordingly. This can in other words help them to adapt their physical contact to the needs of their students. Some students say that when they want to show that they can manage something on their own, that they can do movements or activities by themselves, it is important that the teacher can read such implicit cues from students. Other students say that people are different and that some are more comfortable with physical contact than others. It is very individual, and some students also talk about having different boundaries for different people depending on what you are like as a person. Some people are allowed to get closer to them and some are not, and this has to do with trusting or having faith in a person. In these situations, the teacher's ability to read their students becomes essential for students' experiences.

ii) Student–Teacher Relationship

Closely related to the teacher professionalism theme is the one related to the student–teacher relationship. The relationship between the teacher and students is important in terms of physical contact, since it builds faith and trust between them. It is not only a question of students getting to know their teachers but also the other way around. It is easier to trust a teacher that you have developed a relationship with and with whom one feels familiar with. In one discussion about the use of physical contact, one student says: "It depends on what relationship the teacher has with the students, how kind of close the student feels to the teacher… yeah everything is about, well, trusting the teacher, that matters the most" (male student). The more familiar students feel with the teacher, the easier it is to know what to expect from that teacher.

Good communication between teachers and students also seems to be important for building respectful and trusting relationships. One example of this is a discussion about how physical contact needs to be done in the right way according to students. When asked what that means, students answer that it is difficult to say that physical contact is OK in one situation and not in another and it has to do with communicating with the teacher about how they feel about physical contact. When they feel that they know the teacher, they also trust that the teacher would not do anything to harm them. The relationship between teachers and students is thus very important for the development of a didactic contract concerning physical contact in PE.

iii) Practical Learning

Physical activity is the core of PE in Sweden, and it is mainly a practical subject where students are expected to develop movement abilities. In the light of this it is maybe not surprising that many students agree that in order for them to learn and succeed in PE they sometimes need physical contact from the teacher. It can involve learning new techniques and to understand what muscles to use in a specific movement or activity, or as one student puts it: "I think it is very difficult to learn new techniques if you don't have someone who can help you get a feel for it, so to speak (male student). In other words, it has to do with receiving help in order to accomplish a certain movement. Another example is a student who describes when she learnt how to swim and how the teacher held on to her feet and steered her feet in the correct movement for a breaststroke leg kick. The practical learning aspect is also linked to the teachers' instructive skills and some students claim that they would not always feel safe if the teacher was not there to help them. In addition, the teachers' use of physical contact to prevent injuries is also exemplified. Learning is in these examples clearly related to the teacher's use of physical contact. Students know what to expect and are also dependent on the physical contact from the teacher so that they can learn. If the teacher was not allowed to use physical contact, some students reflect that without physical contact the content of the subject would become quite restricted: "all you can do is running then" (female student). All in all, students expect physical contact from the teacher in order to learn, but also to prevent injuries. This also requires that the teacher can instruct practical subject content in a way that promotes learning, and for some subject contents, this requires the use of physical contact as a pedagogical tool. If the student would not receive the expected physical contact from the teacher, they would no longer be in agreement with the teacher about when, how, or why physical contact is supposed to be used, and the didactic contract would risk being breached. Such breaches could thus have consequences for the student's practical learning.

iv) Teacher Empathic Skills

Another negotiation aspect that students mention are teachers' empathic skills. Students say that they, as children, but also as older teenagers, can need physical contact in PE for encouragement, motivation, comfort, and support. Motivational or encouraging physical contact can for example be a pat on the shoulder or a high five. This kind of physical contact can sometimes mean more to them than just hearing phrases such as "good job": "The teacher can maybe encourage by saying something, but you feel better with a high five…it encourages you more" (male student). Other similar types of physical contact are expressions of happiness, as in a spontaneous hug for scoring a goal. Some also reflect on the need for comfort, as in a hug, if something bad has happened, and that this kind of physical contact from a teacher is also important for them. Several students emphasize that people in general need closeness and that physical contact can be used not only for addressing something that takes place or happens in the gym or in PE but also for human relations and showing care for other people. One student exemplifies this by saying, "Most people need closeness and the teacher is maybe your closest link. Because you don't know what it's like for children at home and such, and then maybe a hug, unwarranted or so, can be good for a child" (female student). Here, the physical contact is not necessarily related to any subject content or any specific events that have taken place in the PE classroom. It is just an expression of care. When students know what they can expect from the teacher, such as help, comfort, and care (and receive it), it is possible to say that a didactic contract has been developed between the teacher and students.

v) Opposite Sex

In general, it is clear that problems related to physical contact can arise when teacher and student are of opposite sex. Especially, this concerns female students and male teachers. Both Swedish students and immigrant students express this but in slightly different ways. The immigrant students often relate the tension between female students and male teachers to their immigrant backgrounds and religious or cultural norms and traditions. The reason for this is that they feel uncertain if physical contact is used as a pedagogical tool or if it means something else. The tension between male teachers and female students is also evident with Swedish female students. It is possible to relate this tension to the strong heteronormativity in Western society. For instance, Swedish female students say that they think more about sex differences the older they get and that a heteronormative tension between men and women arises as children grow into young adults. For these female students, it feels "natural" that a male teacher could be attracted to them as young women. When female students grow older, they gender not only themselves but also male teachers in a heteronormative way. This way of talking can be related to the dominating heteronormative way of talking in society as a whole. The heteronormative discourse thus influences students' view of physical contact in PE.

Another issue that is brought up by all female students is that women are always at risk of being subjected to sexual harassment by men, and that women therefore are cautious around men. At the same time, Swedish female students express sympathy for men and the exposed situation they are in, since they are always under suspicion: "It must be difficult for male teachers too I think…to feel like […] that they are like…not accused…but that they have to be afraid, you know…suspected" (female students). Students clearly sympathize with male teachers who risk being under suspicion of inappropriate behavior, just because they are men. This feeling of sympathy for men can also be related to the power of the heteronormative discourse and specifically the hegemonic position of men over women in society. One interpretation of the female students' feelings of sympathy for men is that they feel inferior to men in general and are therefore more or less "bound" to express these feelings for them. In other words, even though the female students constantly need to deal with the risks of harassment from men, the prevalent heteronormative discourse prescribes them to sympathize with men's vulnerable situation in this case. At the same time, it is evident that the professionalism of the teacher is always of great importance and as long as the teacher acts professionally, it does not really matter if the teacher is male or female. This too reflects a contradiction in terms of physical contact in PE. On the one hand, the male teacher is seen as someone female students need to be somewhat suspicious of, and on the other, the gender of the teacher does not matter as long as they act professionally.

It is also noticeable that the immigrant students feel that there is a difference between different male teachers. Physical contact is more problematic if the male teacher has a similar immigrant background as themselves. These students are worried that such male teachers would look down on them if they did not act in line with the norms and traditions in the similar background, where physical contact between people of different gender is uncommon or even not allowed. Students and teachers with similar immigrant backgrounds may, in other words, not have the same expectations for each other concerning physical contact, and therefore not agree on when, where, or how physical contact can or should be used. In situations like these, it would become more difficult to develop a didactic contract concerning physical contact between teacher and student. It is contradictory that female students, on the one hand, legitimize physical contact due to the teacher's professionalism or the teacher–student relationship and, on the other hand, describe this tension as something that makes them somewhat insecure around male teachers. Contradictions like these make the complexity of physical contact discernible.

Students' reflexivity didactic contracts are developed, recreated, and changed over time. This is not only true for specifically female students or male teachers but is true for all students. It is also clear that students take several negotiation aspects into consideration in the process of developing didactic contracts concerning physical contact with their teachers. Some of these negotiation aspects facilitate this process, while others challenge it. One way of understanding this is that negotiation aspects can work in two ways. For example, if the teacher and student have a good and trusting relationship, or if the student feels that the teacher always acts professionally, this facilitates the process of developing a didactic contract. If, on the other hand, the teacher and student do not have a good relationship or if the student does not feel that the teacher acts professionally, this can instead challenge the development of a didactic contract. From the interviews, it seems that teacher professionalism, the empathic skills of the teacher or the teacher–student relationship generally are good and in accordance with what students expect from their teachers, and as such facilitate the development of a didactic contract. At the same time, opposite gender issues are aspects that rather seem to challenge such as developments. This can be compared to a set of weighing scales, where the weights on one side are students' negotiation aspects that contribute to building trust in the teacher, and those on the other side are aspects that challenge this trust, such as different genders. When students negotiate physical contact, they often take all these aspects into consideration when deciding which side weighs heaviest, that is, they are reflexive in their participation in different learning situations. In a way, this also determines what kind of didactic contract can be developed in relation to physical contact.

Physical contact is often encompassed by implicit norms of what is legitimate physical contact in different situations or with different people. These norms also affect students, teachers, and teaching situations. In different teaching situations, understanding the use and intentions of physical contact is essential for the learning outcome, and also for the development of a didactic contract.

Summary

It has been shown in this chapter how students are reflexive in relation to physical contact in educational settings. Students generally do not analyze or think about physical contact as disconnected from context and confirm that physical contact is a good pedagogical tool. For them, it is the professionalism of the teacher, the relationship the teacher develops with them, and the purpose or intention of physical contact that are relevant and important. At the same time, it is not always as simple as that, and tensions can arise between specifically male teachers and female students.

Physical contact is often used to help students learn practical subject content. There are also occasions when it is used for students' emotional well-being. From a didactical viewpoint, sound relationships between teachers and students cannot be reduced to questions about physical contact per se, as often is the case in policies or guidelines. Physical contact should always be discussed in relation to the specific didactical content, or to the aims of what is being taught. Students have also shown that for them, physical contact is always a part of the context. That is why it is difficult to prescribe or set rules for the use of physical contact because its use is often context sensitive and spontaneously decided upon by the teacher, albeit with the best interests of students and their learning in focus. The negotiation aspects presented here can contribute to the teaching in different educational contexts by discussing alternatives to the one-size-fits-all model, that is, guidelines for appropriate or inappropriate touch. The didactic contract concerns implicit agreements between teachers and students, and here a one-size-fits-all model is not always appropriate. Rather, a teacher's professionalism and ability to read students and situations are of greater value and importance. As such, the didactic contract can offer another, more flexible alternative to discussing physical contact in different educational contexts than the one-size-fits-all model that guidelines and policies offer.

The context-sensitive and often spontaneous use of physical contact by teachers can also be related to what Friesen and Osguthorpe (2018) call tact. They describe tact as: "To quickly sense or know 'the right thing' to do in a particular situation […] to rely on knowledge or sense that is implicit, and even emotional, rather than explicit and logical" (p. 258). One tactful action from a teacher could be the ability to read and interpret students' body language or facial expressions and then decide when or how physical contact ought to be used or not. At a societal level, it is our belief that we need to put more effort into focusing on what teachers do well, instead of searching for a risk-free society. Those who criticize no-touch policies or child safety guidelines do not want to put children at risk. The question is, though, whether adults with an abusive intent will be prevented by such policies or guidelines. Even if these policies and guidelines provide some sense of security, it is unlikely that they will protect all children (Piper, 2015b). We agree with Piper (2015b), who says, "We will not prevent bad people from doing bad things by stopping good people from doing good things" (p. 174). Context-sensitive physical contact could be a better way of ensuring children's safety in PE or sports (see Piper, 2015b). As already indicated, students do not consider physical contact in PE as being disconnected from context. This means that when the purpose or intent of a teacher's use of physical contact is clear, they generally regard it as legitimate. This is important knowledge, considering the evident clash between societal discourses and physical contact as a professional pedagogical tool, and also physical education teacher education (PETE) students' unwillingness to use physical contact in their future teaching, as mentioned in the introduction.

Questions to Discuss

- What does the didactic contract mean, and how can it be used to discuss physical contact between adults and children?
- What negotiation aspects regarding physical contact do you recognize from your own experience as a student, athlete, coach, or teacher?
- Discuss what other negotiation aspects you think students take into account during their school day in general?

CHAPTER 6

The Future – With or Without Physical Contact

The starting point of this book was an example from a gymnastic lesson in our PE teacher education program.[1] Our students were commenting on a physically "touchy" lesson by telling us, "You can't touch pupils today, they might think I am a paedophile, or a 'dirty old man.'" That was, and still is, a frustrating and confusing reality. On the other hand, it reminds us that as a PE teacher or coach you will always be at the crossroads of policy, practice, theory, social media, and social discourses. You will use your own proven experience and the scientific perspectives that your pedagogical means and models resonate. You will embody these and it will set a mark on your personal expression of teaching. It is therefore very hard to reconsider the ways we teach.

The research we refer to in this book shows a tension between the necessity of using physical contact as a pedagogical tool and contemporary discourse which rather supports an avoidance of physical contact. In relation to issues about physical contact, touching or no-touch we nowadays must thoroughly reconsider the way we teach—not because there necessarily is something wrong about the teaching content or what outcome we aspire but because some of our embodied teaching techniques potentially trigs questions about how well we care for our students and ourselves.

In different chapters, we have pointed to how research about intergenerational touch makes evident that how the body is regulated and approached in educational settings have far reaching consequences for teaching and learning outcomes. For example, encounters between teachers and students involve uncertainties in relation to how PE teachers regulate their teaching techniques, and also how students conceive of didactical contracts in the teaching practice and how teachers handle the balance between adaptation to public moral discourse, such as a child protection discourse, and a personal call to teach.

In the prevailing social discourse, physical contact often has sexual connotations. PE teachers are practicing their profession in an environment where they are always potentially at risk of being misinterpreted, and having their pedagogical intent associated with inappropriate behavior or sexual hints. From various perspectives we have illustrated that when our view of educational environments is overly sexualized, it might hamper PE teachers' pedagogical work. Such environments are not conducive to students' learning, development, and growth. Several scholars have explored how the production of a "safe child" and a "safe teacher" has become a dominant feature of everyday work in school. Based on a risk perspective, no touch at all seems to be the solution for creating a "safe child" and a "safe teacher." A right to be protected from sexual or other abuse is indeed a human right for all people. But, if a total avoidance of physical contact is established as a beneficial condition in teaching, where does that lead us? Encouraged by Öhman and Quennerstedt (2017), who explored the more accreditive dimensions of physical contact in relation to a children's rights perspective, we will revisit our initial concerns about physical contact and suggest three forms of work focus that could be developmental for how we regard physical contact in educational settings.

Revisiting Our Initial Concerns

In the introduction of the book, we identified three concerns that, despite being elaborated on in the different chapters, are still evident to the further debate about physical contact. A sound profession will always try to gain from the frustration and disruptions that follow from teachers' everyday work, and it is therefore important to revisit these concerns and reflect on them. In the following, we connect the concerns to three different *work of developments* we think is necessary to adjust teaching and learning to contemporary transformations of educational practices related to physical contact: (i) value-building work, (ii) embodiment work, and (iii) relational work.

Our first concern relates to the self-conception of the PE teachers' profession. When the students after a physically engaging lesson described to us, "You can't touch pupils today, they might think I'm a paedophile or a 'dirty old man,'" we realized that the changes did not come from within the field. The problem rather arose as an amplified sensibility for how we, as a professional group, were looked upon from the outside. In other words, how our professional duties were cross fired by societal discourses and public debates in new ways. The critical view on this is that it points to a corrosion of PE teachers' professionalism. The more hopeful view, though, is that it pushes us, practitioners as well as researchers, to engage more actively in *value-building work* that can strengthen the teachers' profession and make us more grounded in why we are teaching. The teacher/coach professionalism is based on notions of caring, mutual respect, educating young people to engage in positive social and sporting interactions and helping them to become good and caring citizens. When we talk about physical contact and the corrosion of teacher/coach professionalism we believe that both the pedagogy and professional identity are under threat, due to the culture of fear and uncertainty amongst these professionals. They are now under pressure to show appropriate behavior regarding physical contact and avoid problematic incidents. That kind of pressure has in many ways resulted in a paralyzing and defensive practice. Having to constantly ask yourself about appropriate or inappropriate physical contact in your everyday work creates confusion about your own professional identity and the profession. In a way, professionals can now be said to work with a culture of anxiousness instead of a culture of caring, and the professional use of physical contact in PE has come to be viewed as malpractice rather than pedagogy. Against this background the PE teachers' profession, and other occupations where physical contact is used, needs strong value-building work in order to regain action competence. We believe it is important to ask ourselves what kind of society we are creating if physical contact is taboo, and teachers are afraid of touching children. There might be a need to argue the case for "not losing touch."

An important question to ask is which actors should decide how, where and when physical interactions should occur in teaching. Which actors should decide what is appropriate or inappropriate physical contact? Which voices should be heard and listened to? We believe that these actors should not come from outside the world of the education system. If external actors are allowed to intrude on what should be reserved for PE teachers and other professionals with specialist knowledge of how physical contact is used as a pedagogical tool, there is a risk of de-professionalization.

To move forward, we believe that different educational actors, including headmasters, teachers, students, sports club leaders, coaches, athletes, parents, and researchers, need to be involved in the discussions involving physical contact. We firmly believe that it is the actors involved in the education of children and young people that have the experience and knowledge to decide what is needed in the profession and what is educative for children and young people. The agenda should never be dictated by societal trends and fears but must be established on well-grounded professional values, which we must be better equipped to state, discuss, and test. Those of us who have knowledge and experience need to dare to talk about the obviously sensitive subject of physical contact between adults and children in teaching practice. Here, professionals must decide on what role to play in supporting children's and young people's possibilities to experience sufficiently rich and wide experiences of human interactions and relations, and develop confidence in various sports, health, and movement practices. All sport pedagogy environments should be ready to take on this responsibility, and "the touch problem" should be a compulsory part of all education where physical contact is part of the professionals' pedagogical work.

It is only then that we can be free from uncertainty and fear and stand straight-backed in our professional pride.

Our second concern, that the embodied basis for engaging in the PE profession and sport pedagogy has dramatically changed, relates to *embodiment work.* That is, how one of our most familiar pedagogical tools, physical contact, is now threatened. There appears to be a gap between the academic teaching culture at the university and the more practical teaching conditions at the schools and sport clubs. This means that we can not only address physical contact as an internal professional value project. Grounded professional values are still important, but to bridge this gap, they must be sophistically operationalized into teaching tools and habits that are more readily adapted to the teaching conditions in schools and sport clubs.

One way to approach this is to establish physical contact as a content in its own right in our university educations and sports programs. Students and athletes are extensively taught about the body (anatomy, physiology, movement, etc.), but it is also important to bring in learning content about physical contact between people. For example, we can design teaching units that focus on the tacit knowledge of how to navigate the space of intimacy in teacher–student and coach–athlete encounters and relationships. Inspirations to such designs can be found, in this book, in relation to perceptual awareness and how we make sure that our adjusted teaching techniques do not reduce bodily displacement to something sexual or establish physical contact as the equivalent to sexual attempts. The connection between perceptual awareness and teaching techniques can also be exemplified through different experiences between, for example, "feeling the teacher's body" and "feeling one's own body" when being physically touched in an instructional situation. In this context, physical contact needs to be focused on whether a technique of bodily touch is effectively reproduced and has its intended outcomes, to what extent it transmits the important values connected to it, how it can be developed based on novel purposes or alternatively disappear when confronted with no-touch discourses. The embodiment work researchers and practitioners must do here is to explore and discuss if techniques of bodily touch can be reproduced against the background of traditional embodied intentions, be combined with novel intentions, or should be discontinued as techniques.

Our third concern relates to PE teachers *relational work* and the ability to critically adopt both a teacher and student perspective on physical contact. This stems from how we began to realize that the younger generation of sports pedagogues and teachers were worried about being mistrusted or accused of sexual harassment. Our university students' unwillingness to use physical contact in their future teaching, as well as the evident clash between certain societal discourses and physical contact as a professional pedagogical tool, led us to reinforce a clearer student perspective on physical contact. Here, we must know more about how students in the schools experience physical contact in teaching situations, and in what ways students' and teachers' experiences about vulnerability and anxiety overlap and differ. Such knowledge can, furthermore, help us to address our third concern in terms of how we can build lasting and mutual relationships between teachers and students. Our own research shows that students generally do not analyze or think about physical contact as disconnected from context and confirm that physical contact is a good pedagogical tool. For them, it is the professionalism of the teacher, the relationship the teacher develops with them, and the purpose or intention of physical contact that are relevant and important. At the same time, it is also indicated that it is not always as simple as that, and that tensions can arise between specifically male teachers and female students. Again, to address the worries of being mistrusted, robust relational work must be on the agenda for teachers to regain their professional action competence. As we have mentioned before, this is a matter of communication, that is, daring to talk about and discuss this seemingly sensitive topic. The more silent we become, the more suspicion is created.

Closing Notes

Twenty years ago, Piper and Smith (2003, p. 890) made the observation that "A moral panic has led to the production of guidelines that are concerned with protecting children from abuse and adults from false allegations, but where the needs of children are lost." Against the background of our three major concerns, we have tried to explore the different conditions, perspectives, and challenges that surround Piper and Smith's observation. By summing these up here, we also suggest three forms of actions that researchers and practitioners should focus on: value work, embodiment work, and relational work. Through these suggested forms of actions, we believe we have the possibility to ground teaching and coaching as caring professions, while never succumbing to thoughtless and senseless adaptation to public moral discourses.

The book can be seen as a tool to be used to critically evaluate and discuss how public moral discourses intervenes or supports teachers' and sports pedagogues' continuously work on grounding their professions in certain values, embodied teaching, and relationships. We hope that the book contains the arguments and the examples needed to inform academic and professional discussions about how teaching and learning can adjust to contemporary transformations of social practices related to physical contact. In each chapter, we have asked didactic questions that are important to discuss for all parties and at all levels in educational systems and training programs. While not diminishing the importance of dealing with problems of abuse, harm, and sexual harassment, we do want to emphasize critical consequences of "no touch," and the need for reflections and alternative perspectives on physical contact in educational settings.

Parallel to the rise of intergenerational touch as a research field we have seen PE and sports pedagogy adopting new teaching and learning content in other areas. For example, the sports pedagogy literature is rich in studies of meaningfulness, yoga, mindfulness, artistic expression, and aesthetic experience. Together, such perspectives broaden our view of PE and sport and help establish new forms of training and movement learning activities. The means, experiences, and outcomes of these activities connect to new purposes and aims in schools and sports clubs, and, of course, have consequences on how we approach issues around physical contact. One obvious question according to this development is if these "new" forms mean less or more use of physical contact as a pedagogical tool? If the forms, processes, and contents of PE and sports pedagogy change, teacher/coaches and students/athletes must negotiate new didactical contracts which also means we have to keep track on student/athlete perspectives and how these might transform. In relation to the negotiation of didactical contracts, it is crucial to also explore how the body is constituted and regulated at different places and times during students' and athletes' everyday school or sports club lives. In this regard, sports and coaching environments may face different challenges compared to school environments.

So, should we, as teachers and sports pedagogues, stop touching our students and athletes? From a pedagogical perspective there is no absolute answer to that question. Many of the worries about physical contact being misinterpreted as something sexual holds true for inappropriate non-touch behavior too. With or without physical contact, caring professions that revolve around pedagogical aims will always be practiced with a certain risk of being misinterpreted and misunderstood.

As PE teachers, preschool teachers, sports coaches, or professionals in other occupations where physical contact is used, we have beliefs, desires, and feelings in our everyday work. We are trying to shape skills, knowledge, values, and persons. In that process, we use our embodied selves, and with great engagement and with some luck, the outcome can be described as art, but we are not solitary artists in this process; the success relies on how well we work together with students, athletes, or children in that process, and to what extent we can share important experiences and situations with them. In this way, we all are part of the same art. This is what makes the issue of physical contact between adults and children in educational settings so much more complex. It appears that we need to create didactic contracts that we share and trust with each other. Otherwise, there is a risk that our teaching will result in bad habits that lead us away from the routes that can realize our educational vision and our call to teach.

The broadest conclusion we dare to make here is that researchers and practitioners must be better at recognizing the complexity of pedagogical intent, while never stopping working to make it as visible and communicative as possible. Our future value-building work, embodiment work, and relational work depend on it. So does the students' and athletes' learning and growth. All this important work involves discussions about interpersonal touch, physical contact, and trust.

Further Readings

In the book, we have used some theoretical concepts. The concept of discourse helps us to understand the different perspectives on physical contact in educational settings and the consequences it has for the pedagogical work of teachers and coaches. The changing pedagogical techniques that teachers develop can be understood in terms of self-governance, that is, that the teachers control their actions in line with the prevailing discourse. Further reading about these discursive perspectives can be found in:

- Öhman, M., & Quennerstedt, A. (2017). Questioning the no-touch discourse in physical education from a children's rights perspective. *Sport, Education and Society, 22*(3), 305–320.
  This article questions the rationality of "no-touch policies" from a children's rights perspective and offers an alternative approach to the matter of physical contact between teachers and students in the context of physical education (PE) in schools.
- Öhman, M. (2017). Losing touch–Teachers' self-regulation in physical education. *European Physical Education Review, 23*(3), 297–310.

This article takes its starting point in the discourse of child protection and the growing anxiety around intergenerational touch in educational settings. The article shows PE teachers' self-regulation in relation to the child protection discourse and no-touch policies.

The concepts of body pedagogy and teaching as a caring profession are developed from a tradition of classical pragmatism and contribute with an actor-oriented perspective about physical contact, that is, how we can recognize certain habits and techniques that teachers and sports pedagogues value within a certain educational setting, as well as how these habits and techniques are results of reciprocal relationships between teachers, students, environments, and societal discourses. For further reading about these pedagogical perspectives, we suggest the following books:

- Garrison, J. (2010). *Dewey and Eros: Wisdom and desire in the art of teaching*. IAP.
  The fundamental lesson in Garrison's book is that teachers desire to call into existence the good of their practice, which also means that they have to call into existence the good of their students. Although not focusing on physical contact it contains distinct arguments of how we as teachers and pedagogues can make careful choices in educational settings.
- Shilling, C. (2016). *The Body: A very short introduction.* Oxford University Press.
  For teachers and sports pedagogues to be well grounded in their choices about physical contact in educational settings it is crucial to be informed about the connections between bodies and social relations. In this accessible version of different perspectives on the meaning of the body Shilling explains and discusses how bodies are important practical

as well as intellectual matters where thought and action occur through our embodied being.

The didactic contract is a theoretical concept that can be used to understand student's perspectives of physical contact in PE. The didactic contract implies an unspoken agreement in the relationship between teachers and students in teaching practice. As a concept, it facilitates critical questions about the confidence that must be established between teacher and student to make learning possible, and how that process relates to physical contact as a teaching phenomenon. For example, when is the didactic contract at risk of being broken in situations where physical contact occurs? Further reading about the didactic contract and students' perspectives of physical contact can be found in:

- Caldeborg, A. (2021). *Physical contact in physical education: New perspectives and future directions.* (Örebro Studies in Sport Science 33). [Dissertation, Örebro University], Örebro University, Repro 05/2021.
  This doctoral thesis focuses on students' perspectives of physical contact in PE. It also explores the theoretical concept of the didactic contract.
- Caldeborg, A. (2022). Physical contact in physical education—Immigrant students' perspectives. *Sport, Education and Society, 27*(1), 72–84. https://doi.org/10.1080/13573322.2020.1816539
  This article focuses on immigrant students' perspectives of physical contact in PE. It shows that students take several different negotiation aspects into account in determining if physical contact from the teacher is regarded as legitimate or not by the students.

NOTES

Chapter 1

1. The examples that are used in this book draw partly on interview data from the project: *Don't touch!— Pedagogical consequences of the "forbidden" body in Physical Education.* The project was funded by the Swedish National Centre for Research in Sports. The examples also draw on interview data from the doctoral thesis project: Physical contact in *physical education: New perspectives and future directions.*

Chapter 2

1. This chapter is a rework of the article Caldeborg, A., Andersson, J., & Öhman, M. (2023). Physical contact in physical education, sports coaching and the preschool—A scoping review. *Sport, Education and Society, 28*(3), 326–340.

Chapter 3

1. This chapter is a rework of the articles: Öhman, M., & Quennerstedt, A. (2017). Questioning the no-touch discourse in physical education from a children's rights perspective. *Sport, Education and Society, 22*(3), 305–320; Öhman, M. (2017). Losing touch–Teachers' self-regulation in physical education. *European Physical Education Review, 23*(3), 297–310.
2. For a deeper discussion of this complexity, see the special edition of *Sport, Education and Society* entitled "Hands off! The practice, policy, and politics of touch in sport and educational settings" (Piper et al., 2013a, 2013b), and also the book *Touch in sports coaching and physical education* (Piper, 2015a).
3. The examples that are used in this book draw partly on interview data from the project: *Don't touch!—Pedagogical consequences of the "forbidden" body in Physical Education.* The project was funded by the Swedish National Centre for Research in Sports. The examples also draw on interview data from the doctoral thesis project: *Physical contact in physical education: New perspectives and future directions.*

Chapter 4

1. This chapter is a rework of the article: Andersson, J., Öhman, M., & Garrison, J. (2018). Physical education teaching as a caring act—Techniques of bodily touch and the paradox of caring. *Sport, Education and Society, 23(6),* 591–606.

Chapter 5

1. This chapter is a rework of the articles Caldeborg, A., Maivorsdotter, N., & Öhman, M. (2019). Touching the didactic contract—A student perspective on intergenerational touch in PE. *Sport, Education and Society, 24*(3), 256–268; Caldeborg, A. (2022). Physical contact in physical education–immigrant students' perspectives. *Sport, Education and Society, 27*(1), 72–84; Caldeborg, A., & Öhman, M. (2020). Intergenerational touch in physical education in relation to heteronormativity: Female students' perspectives. *European Physical Education Review, 26*(2), 392–409.

Chapter 6

1. Even though all examples in the book are taken from the school subject Physical Education, they are also relevant for other areas, for example, teachers of other school subjects, preschool teachers, sports coaches, or professionals in other occupations where physical contact is essential, such as nurses and carers for older people. In the text, however, we use teachers more often to make the text more straightforward.

REFERENCES

Åberg, M., Hedlin, M., & Johansson, C. (2019). Preschool anxieties: Constructions of risk and gender in preschool teachers' talk on physical interaction with children. *Journal of Early Childhood Research, 17*(2), 104–115. https://doi.org/10.1177/1476718X18816347

Amade-Escot, C. (2000). The contribution of Two Research Programs on Teaching Content: "Pedagogical Content Knowledge" and "Didactics of Physical Education." *Journal of Teaching in Physical Education, 20*, 78–101.

Amade-Escot, C. (2006). Student learning within the *Didactique* tradition. In D. Kirk, D. Macdonald, & M. O'Sullivan (Eds.), *The handbook of physical education* (pp. 347–365). Sage Publications.

Amade-Escot, C. (2017). How gender order is enacted in Physical Education: The didactique approach. In G. Doll-Tepper, K. Koenen, & R. Bailey (Eds.), *Sport, education and social policy: The state of the social sciences of sport* (pp. 62–79. Routledge.

Andersson, J., Öhman, M., & Garrison, J. (2018). Physical education teaching as a caring act—Techniques of bodily touch and the paradox of caring. *Sport, Education and Society, 23*(6), 591–606. https://doi.org/10.1080/13573322.2016.1244765

Andrzejewski, C. E., & Davis, H. A. (2008). Human contact in the classroom: Exploring how teachers talk about and negotiate touching students. *Teaching and Teacher Education, 24*(3), 779–794. https://doi.org/10.1016/j.tate.2007.02.013

Bignante, E. (2010). The use of photo-elicitation in field research—Exploring Maasai representations and use of natural resources. *EchoGéo, 11*, 1–20. https://doi.org/10.4000/echogeo.11622

Brackenridge, C. (2001). *Spoilsports: Understanding and preventing sexual exploitation in sport*. Routledge.

Brousseau, G. (1997). Theory of didactical situations in mathematics. In Balacheff, N., Cooper, M., Sutherland, R., & Warfield, V. (Eds.), *Theory of didactical situations in mathematics*. Kluwer Academic Publishers.

Caldeborg, A. (2021). *Physical contact in physical education: New perspectives and future directions* (Doctoral dissertation, Örebro University).

Caldeborg, A. (2022). Physical contact in physical education—Immigrant students' perspectives. *Sport, Education and Society, 27*(1), 72–84.

Caldeborg, A., Andersson, J., & Öhman, M. (2023). Physical contact in physical education, sports coaching and the preschool—A scoping review. *Sport, Education and Society, 28*(3), 326–340.

Caldeborg, A., & Öhman, M. (2020). Intergenerational touch in physical erducation in relation to heteronormativity: Female studnets' perspectives. *European Physical Education Review, 26*(2), 392–409.

Evans, J., Davies, B., & Rich, E. (2009). The body made flesh: Embodied learning and the corporeal device. *British Journal of Sociology of Education, 30*(4), 391–406.

Fasting, K. (2005). Research on sexual harassment and abuse in sport. *Idrottsforum.org*. [*Nordic Sport Science Forum*]. Retrieved November 6, 2020, at idrottsforum.org 2005-04-05.

Fletcher, S. (2013). Touching practice and physical education: Deconstruction of a contemporary moral panic. *Sport, Education and Society, 18*(5), 694–709. https://doi.org/10.1080/13573322.2013.774272

Foucault, M. (1991). Truth and power. In Paul Rabinow (Ed.), *The Foucault reader* (pp. 51–75). Penguin Books. (Original work published 1978).

Foucault, M. (2002). The subject and power. In James D. Faubion (Ed.), *Essential works of Foucault 1954–1984*. (Vol. 3, Power, pp. 324, 326–348). Penguin Books. (Original work published 1982).

Friesen, N., & Osguthorpe, R. (2018). Tact and the pedagogical triangle: The authenticity of teachers in relation. *Teaching and Teacher Education, 70*, 255–264. https://doi.org/10.4102/hts.v73i1.3864

Garratt, D., Piper, H., & Taylor, B. (2013). "Safeguarding" sports coaching: Foucault, genealogy and critique. *Sport, Education and Society, 18*(5), 615–629. https://doi.org/10.1080/13573322.2012.736861

Garrison, J. (2010). *Dewey and Eros: Wisdom and desire in the art of teaching*. IAP.

Gundem, B. B. (2011). *Europeisk didaktikk, tenkning og viten*. Universitetsforlaget.

Hall, S. (2004). Foucault: Power, knowledge and discourse. In M. Whetherell, S. Taylor, & S. Yates (Eds.), *Discourse theory and practice: A reader* (pp. 72–81). Sage Publications.

Hedlin, M. (2021). "Nu är man betydligt mer försiktig": Förskollärare om den fysiska kontakten mellan pedagoger och barn ["Today we are much more careful": Preschool teachers on the physical contact between educators and children]. *Barn—forskning om barn og barndom i Norden, 39*(1), 1–16. https://doi.org/10.5324/barn.v39i1.3397

Johnson, R. (2015). Training "safe" bodies in an era of child panic in the United States: New technologies for disciplining the self. In H. Piper (Ed.), *Touch in sports coaching and physical education: Fear, risk and moral panic* (pp. 35–51). Routledge.

Jones, A. (2004). Social anxiety, sex, surveillance and the "safe" teachers. *British Journal of Sociology of Education, 25*(1), 53–66.

Jones, R., Bailey, J., & Santos, S. (2013). Coaching, caring and the politics of touch: A visual exploration. *Sport, Education and Society, 18*(5), 648–662. https://doi.org/10.1080/13573322.2013.769945

Jung, H., & Choi, E. (2016). The importance of indirect teaching behaviour and its educational effects in physical education. *Physical Education and Sport Pedagogy, 21*(2), 121–136. https://doi.org/10.1080/17408989.2014.923990

Kempe, H., Silverman, F., Steele, B., Droegmuller, W., & Silver, H. (1985). The Battered-Child Syndrome. *Child Abuse and Neglect, 9*, 143–154.

Lawrence, A. (2004). *Principles of child protection: Management and practice*. Open University Press.

Lyons, K. (2014). She'll be right? An Australian perspective on caring for young people in physical education and sport. In H. Piper (Ed.), *Touch in sports coaching and physical education: Fear, risk and moral panic* (pp. 135–150). Routledge.

McCuaig, L. A., Ohman, M., & Wright, J. (2013). Shepherds in the gym: Employing a pastoral power analytic on caring teaching in HPE. *Sport, Education and Society, 18*(6), 788–806.

McWilliam, E., & Jones, A. (2005). An unprotected species? On teachers as risky subjects. *British Educational Research Journal, 31*(1), 109–120.

Miller, M. (2012). The role of service-learning to promote early childhood physical education while examining its influence upon the vocational call to teach. *Physical Education and Sport Pedagogy, 17*(1), 61–77. https://doi.org/10.1080/17408981003712810

Nealon, J. (2008). *Foucault beyond Foucault: Power and its intensifications since 1984*. Stanford University Press.

References

Öhman, M. (2017). Losing touch—Teachers' self-regulation in physical education. *European Physical Education Review, 23*(3), 297–310. https://doi.org/10.1177/1356336X15622159

Öhman, M., & Grundberg Sandell, C. (2015). The pedagogical consequences of "no touching" in physical education: The case of Sweden. In H. Piper (Ed.), *Touch in sports coaching and physical education: Fear, risk and moral panic* (pp. 70–84). Routledge.

Öhman, M., & Quennerstedt, A. (2017). Questioning the no-touch discourse in physical education from a children's rights perspective. *Sport, Education and Society, 22*(3), 305–320. https://doi.org/10.1080/13573322.2015.1030384

Owens, L., & Ennis, C. (2005). The ethic of care in teaching: An overview of supportive literature. *Quest, 57*(4), 392–425.

Piper, H. (2015a). *Touch in sports coaching and physical education: Fear, risk and moral panic*. Routledge.

Piper, H. (2015b). Fear, risk, and child protection in sport. In H. Piper (Ed.), *Touch in sports coaching and physical education: Fear, risk and moral panic* (pp. 167–186). Routledge.

Piper, H., Garratt, D., & Taylor, B. (2013a). Hands off! The practice and politics of touch in physical education and sports coaching. *Sport, Education and Society, 18*(5), 575–582.

Piper, H., Garratt, D., & Taylor, B. (2013b). Child abuse, child protection, and defensive "touch" in PE teaching and sports coaching. *Sport, Education and Society, 18*(5), 583–598.

Piper, H., & Smith, H. (2003). "Touch" in educational and child care settings: Dilemmas and responses. *British Educational Research Journal, 29*(6), 879–894.

Piper, H., & Stronach, I. (2008). *Don't touch! The educational story of a panic*. Routledge.

Piper, H., Taylor, W. G., & Garratt, D. (2012). Sports coaching in risk society: No touch! No trust! *Sport, Education and Society, 17*(3), 331–345. https://doi.org/10.1080/13573322.2011.608937

Quennerstedt, M., & Larsson, H. (2015). Learning moving cultures in physical education. *Sport, Education and Society, 20*(5), 565–572. https://doi.org/10.1080/13573322.2014.994490

Rose, N. (1999). *Powers of freedom: Reframing political thought*. Cambridge University Press.

Sarrazy, B., & Novotná, J. (2013). Didactical contract and responsiveness to didactical contract: A theoretical framework for enquiry into students' creativity in mathematics. *ZDM Mathematics Education, 45*, 281–293. https://doi.org/10.1007/s11858-013-0496-4

Shilling, C. (2007). Sociology and the body: Classical traditions and new agendas. *The Sociological Review, 55*(s1), 1–18.

Shilling, C. (2008). *Changing bodies: Habit, crisis and creativity*. London: SAGE.

Shilling, C. (2022). Body pedagogics, transactional identities and human–animal relations. *Sociology, 56*(4), 766–782.

Steckley, L. (2012). Touch, physical restraint and therapeutic containment in residential child care. *British Journal of Social Work, 42*(3), 537–555.

Svinth, L. (2018). Being touched—The transformative potential of nurturing touch practices in relation to toddlers' learning and emotional well-being. *Early Child Development and Care, 188*(7), 924–936. https://doi.org/10.1080/03004430.2018.1446428

Taylor, W. G., Piper, H., & Garratt, D. (2016). Sports coaches as "dangerous individuals"—practice as governmentality. *Sport, Education and Society, 21*(2), 183–199. https://doi.org/10.1080/13573322.2014.899492

Toftegaard Nielsen, J. (2001). The Forbidden Zone: Intimacy, sexual relations and misconduct in the relationship between coaches and athletes. *International Review for the Sociology of Sport, 36*(2), 165–182.

Varea, V., & Öhman, M. (2023). "Break the rules or quit the job": Physical education teachers' experiences of physical contact in their teaching practice. *Sport, Education and Society, 28*(4), 395–406.

Verscheure, I., & Amade-Escot, C. (2007). The gendered construction of physical education content as the result of the differentiated didactic contract. *Physical Education and Sport Pedagogy, 12*(3), 245–272. https://doi.org/10.1080/17408980701610185

Winther-Jörgensen, M., & Philips, L. (2000). *Diskursanalys som teori och metod.* Studentlitteratur.

The World Organization of the Scout Movement European Region/World Association of Girl Guides and Girl Scouts. (2007). *Child Protection Tool Kit: A joint project of the WSB—European Regional Office and the Europe Region WAGGGS.* Author.

www.ingramcontent.com/pod-product-compliance
Lightning Source LLC
Chambersburg PA
CBHW030052170426
43197CB00010B/1489